SNAPREVISE

SnapRevise Text Guide:
The Tempest
by William Shakespeare

Darcy Campbell

InStudent Education UK Ltd owner of SnapRevise® trademark.
43 Priston Close, Worle, BS22 7FL, Weston-Super-Mare, United Kingdom

www.snaprevise.co.uk

Copyright © InStudent Publishing Pty Ltd 2024

All rights reserved. These notes are protected by copyright owned by InStudent Publishing Pty Ltd and you may not reproduce, disseminate, or communicate to the public the whole or a substantial part thereof except as permitted at law or with the prior written consent of InStudent Publishing Pty Ltd.

Title: The Tempest by William Shakespeare Text Guide
ISBN: 978-1-917424-47-9

Published by InStudent Education UK Ltd CN 15550989 under licence from InStudent Publishing Pty Ltd.
ACN 624 188101

Disclaimer
No reliance on warranty. These SnapRevise materials are intended to supplement but are not intended to replace or to be any substitute for your regular school attendance, for referring to prescribed texts, or for your own note taking. You are responsible for following the appropriate syllabus, attending school classes, and maintaining good study practices. It is your responsibility to evaluate the accuracy of any information, opinions, and advice in these materials. Under no circumstance will InStudent Publishing Pty Ltd or InStudent Education UK Ltd ("Publishers"), their officers, agents, or employees be liable for any loss or damage caused by your use or reliance on these materials, including any adverse impact upon your performance in any academic subject as a result of your use or reliance on the materials. You accept that all information provided or made available by the Publishers is in the nature of general information and does not constitute advice. It is not guaranteed to be error-free and you should always independently verify any information, including through use of a professional teacher and other reliable resources. To the extent permissible at law, the Publishers expressly disclaim all warranties or guarantees of any kind, whether express or implied, including without limitation any warranties concerning the accuracy or content of information provided in these materials or other fitness for purpose. The Publishers shall not be liable for any direct, indirect, special, incidental, consequential or punitive damages of any kind. You agree to indemnify the Publishers, its officers, agents, and employees against any loss whatsoever by using these materials.

Preface

Hi! My name is Darcy Campbell and I am currently studying a Bachelor of Arts/Bachelor of Advanced Studies, majoring in Politics and International Relations and History as a Dalyell Scholar at the University of Sydney.

But beyond that, the most important thing you need to know is that I'm a *massive* Shakespeare fan! However, it's certainly taken me a while to get to this point, so I completely understand if you're a little hesitant about studying *The Tempest* and only picked up this Text Guide because you're struggling to love/understand/appreciate the play.

I came to love Shakespeare through acting in several of his plays and seeing his magic performed live. There's a quality to Shakespeare (especially *The Tempest),* which doesn't quite shine through until actors led by an innovative director breathe new life into Shakespeare's centuries-old words.

Fortunately, I was one such actor in a recent production of *The Tempest* and through my experience with the play I realised the sheer joy and depth of *The Tempest* and its characters. I saw the electricity spark between Prospero and Caliban in a more meaningful way than ever before, and came to understand the comedic genius of Gonzalo. I laughed more than I had simply reading the play word-for-word on page, and I teared up at poignant moments which I hadn't fully conceptualised until I saw them on the stage.

I hope in these pages to capture that same magic for you and to take you into the divine, mystical, and wild world of Shakespeare's final work.

See you on the island!

— Darcy Campbell

Contents

1. **Nutshell Summary** ... 1
2. **Background Information** ... 3
   - Shakespeare's authorship ... 3
   - Jacobean society ... 4
3. **Scene-by-Scene Analysis** ... 5
   - Act 1 Scene 1 ... 5
   - Act 1 Scene 2 ... 5
   - Act 2 Scene 1 ... 11
   - Act 2 Scene 2 ... 13
   - Act 3 Scene 3 ... 14
   - Act 3 Scene 2 ... 15
   - Act 3 Scene 3 ... 16
   - Act 4 Scene 1 ... 18
   - Act 5 Scene 1 ... 19
4. **Character Analysis** ... 24
   - Prospero ... 24
   - Miranda ... 25
   - Ariel ... 26
   - Caliban ... 27
   - Ferdinand ... 28
   - Alonso ... 29
   - Gonzalo ... 29
   - Antonio and Sebastian ... 29
   - Stephano and Trinculo ... 30
   - Mariners, spirits, and other courtiers ... 30
5. **Key Themes Analysis** ... 31
   - Power ... 31
   - Reality vs. illusions ... 31
   - Imprisonment ... 32
   - Discovery ... 32
   - Language ... 33
   - Revenge and forgiveness ... 33
6. **Structural Features Analysis** ... 34
   - Setting ... 34
   - Binaries ... 34
   - Classical unities ... 35
   - Motifs ... 36
     - Magic ... 36
     - Music ... 36

7 Quote Bank   **37**
   Power and control 37
   Family 38
   Ambition 38
   Discovery 38
   Love and marriage 39
   Morality 39
   Revenge and forgiveness 40
   Language 41
   Magic and illusions 41
   Loss 42

8 Sample Essays   **43**
   Essay One 43
   Essay Two 48
   Essay Three 53
   Essay Four 58

Section 1

Nutshell Summary

The Tempest begins, conveniently enough, with a **tempest**. The courtiers – the main ones being Alonso (the King of Naples), Ferdinand (Alonso's son), Antonio (the Duke of Milan), Gonzalo (adviser to the King), and Sebastian (the brother of the King) – are on board a ship with the Mariners and Boatswain. The storm worsens and chaos ensues.

Tempest: a violent, raging storm.

The conductor of the storm is then revealed – the wronged Duke of Milan, Prospero, who after being **usurped** by his brother Antonio, King Alonso, and Sebastian, fled to the island which he and his daughter, Miranda, now live on. After years of keeping her in the dark, Prospero decides *now* is the time to tell Miranda of their past seeing as the storm "hath mine enemies / Brought to this shore." He then calls his spirit/servant Ariel to the stage and bids him to report on the shipwreck they have just caused together. Ariel recounts the tale of the shipwreck with sheer delight, and reports that all of the royal party are in fact safe upon the shore with "not a hair perished." After Ariel gets a little bit volatile, Prospero awakens Miranda and off they go to visit Caliban – the 'monster' which Prospero has imprisoned within the rocks. It's revealed that Caliban is furious with Prospero and resents his capture, which will eventually lead to his usurping desires later in the play.

Usurped: to have one's position seized from them.

Next, Ariel brings Ferdinand to Prospero and Miranda, and since Ferdinand is the first man that Miranda has ever seen except her father and Caliban, she instantly falls in love. He promises that he'll make her Queen of Naples and off the happy couple go.

The other courtiers (who Ferdinand believes are drowned!) enter and become absolutely enthralled by the island, confused by its music, wonders, and mystique. Their scenes mostly consist of good-natured Gonzalo trying to cheer up poor Alonso who believes that his son is drowned, as they wander confused around the island. But while Alonso mopes (and naps), Antonio and Sebastian rile each other up to kill Alonso and thereby transfer the throne to Sebastian, seeing as Alonso's heirs are gone (with Ferdinand believed to be drowned, and Claribel married to the King of Tunis).

We are then introduced to the final set of characters, Trinculo and Stephano, two lower class members of the courtier party. After getting mixed up with Caliban, who proclaims them his new masters, they decide to murder Prospero and take the isle for themselves.

Meanwhile, as Ferdinand and Miranda fall deeper in love (and eventually get married!), Prospero and Ariel haunt and taunt the courtiers drawing them not only closer to Prospero, but closer to the brink of insanity. Eventually, just before meeting with his enemies (both the usurpers of his past and of his present), Prospero decides to part with his magic and rather than pursue revenge, decides upon forgiveness.

Upon Prospero revealing himself to them, the courtiers are dumbstruck. Alonso in particular is so affected by both seeing Prospero and the horrors he has experienced on the island that he immediately revokes the Dukedom from Antonio and restores it to Prospero. Prospero **indicts** Antonio and Sebastian for their immoral actions before revealing to Alonso that not only is his son Ferdinand alive, he is healthy and in love with Prospero's daughter Miranda.

Indict: to formally accuse someone of committing a crime.

After the happy reunion between father and son, Ariel brings the new usurpers (Caliban, Trinculo, and Stephano) to Prospero and they apologise for their actions. For Ariel's obedience, Prospero decides to set him free, but Caliban's future is unclear. While Prospero and Miranda will be travelling back to Italy with the courtiers, Shakespeare leaves us in the dark regarding Caliban's fate, ending with a grand epilogue delivered by Prospero, begging the audience to release not just Prospero from his role, but the actor too.

Section 2
Background Information

Alright, before we can dive into a scene-by-scene analysis, let's go through a bit of background info!

Shakespeare's authorship

The play was probably written sometime in either 1610 or 1611 and was the last play written solely by Shakespeare (as opposed to those he co-authored before his death: *Henry VIII* and *The Two Noble Kingsmen* before his death in 1616).

Another interesting point to note is that it was also one of Shakespeare's only plays in which the plot is *completely original*. A lot of his other plays, like *Hamlet,* took inspiration from other sources, most notably the plays of his contemporary Christopher Marlowe, and *Holinshed's Chronicles* which was a historical record of British history. However, *The Tempest* is all from the mind of Shakespeare, except for a few references to the travel literature of his time.

The most important contextual influence on the way we should read this play is the **dominance of Western colonisation in Shakespeare's time**. In the 17th century, the European colonial project was well under way, with Europeans (especially Britons) spreading their influence/taking land all over the world. The theme of **discovery and travel** is clearly very important to the play, whether we read it through a **post-colonial lens** or not, given the plot's focus on a shipwreck with a royal family on board on the way back to Italy from Tunis, especially given the courtiers end up on an island in the middle of the ocean!

But beyond themes of travel and discovery, the dominance of colonisation at the time also has an impact on the way we should view the power relations on the island. Caliban, portrayed by Shakespeare as a monster, would have been identified by the audience of the time as a stereotypical 'savage.' Caliban, the rightful owner of the island, is treated poorly by everyone who visits the island and he quickly assumes a subservient role to anyone who exerts their control. Furthermore, even Caliban's ability to speak English encourages us to question the colonial dynamics: is learning English a good thing if it's just used to then control Caliban? In addition to Caliban, the colonial context seems to infiltrate the minds of all the characters in the play – *even* the good guy Gonzalo muses about what he would do on the island if it was his.

Colonisation: the process of taking control of land belonging to Indigenous people, and expanding imperial powers.

Post-colonial: a literary term for interpreting texts by thinking about the issues and consequences of colonialism in a work of literature.

Swansong: the final performance in someone's career.

Homage: a demonstration of respect or acknowledgement.

Another thing we should be aware of before we get cracking is the debate which surrounds *The Tempest* being **Shakespeare's swansong.** While we can't ever know for sure what Shakespeare was intending to do with *The Tempest* (trying to figure out the motives of a dead person is never a feasible task), we *can* read *The Tempest* in light of it being his final play, a reading which delivers us a multiplicity of meanings. If we read it as Shakespeare's farewell to the theatre, Prospero's character can be interpreted as **a homage to the artist himself.** Rather than simply a critique of power and manipulation, Prospero's character can be viewed as a playwright struggling to let go of *his* magic – the magic of the pen.

Jacobean society

Humanism: a philosophy that values individual agency and rationality over blind adherence to religious beliefs.

And finally, we should consider the influence of the social and cultural context of the Elizabethan/Jacobean world on *The Tempest*. The play deals with many of the themes Shakespeare had rigorously pursued throughout his career – power, love, control, monarchical rule, the struggle between religion and **humanism**... the list could go on forever! These themes were all pertinent in Shakespeare's time due to England's struggle to come to terms with the ruling and power politics of the state. While other plays have dealt with power politics in a more explicit form (*Hamlet*, for example, directly uses a royal setting to critique royal power), *The Tempest* presents a **subtler, more pervasive criticism of the uses and abuses of power in his time.**

Furthermore, considering the social and cultural context of England at the time is important to understanding **how the audience would have reacted** to a major theme of the play: **magic!** In Shakespeare's world, the lines between magic and reality were a little more blurred than they are today. It was commonplace to believe in superstitions and spirits and charms, so Prospero's wielding of magic at the time would have been considered a serious force for justice (or injustice) rather than just hocus pocus nonsense.

Now that we have a broad understanding of Shakespeare's world and the way in which *The Tempest* fits into it, let's get this party started!

Section 3

Scene-by-Scene Analysis

Act 1 Scene 1

This scene is nice and short, but don't think for a *second* that this means it lacks significance! This scene introduces the audience to the sheer power of Prospero's magic, even though they don't know it yet. The actual tempest or shipwrecking is reimagined by directors all the time, but the one thing each reinterpretation tends to have in common is that the scene is meant to strike **fear, wonder, amazement,** or a combination of all three into the hearts of the audience. Immediately, we are exposed the grandeur of Prospero and the magic of the isle, thus setting up a play literally called *The Tempest* nicely.

The scene also has a lot to reveal to us about the courtiers. The ship is returning from the marriage of King Alonso's daughter Claribel to the King of Tunis. On board the ship are the king himself, his brother Sebastian, his advisor Gonzalo, his son Ferdinand, and the new Duke of Milan, Antonio (who usurped his own brother, Prospero), as well as a whole cast of mariners and other lesser courtiers such as Stephano and Trinculo.

As the ship goes down, good-natured Gonzalo just wants everyone to survive, whereas Sebastian and Antonio reveal their **maliciousness.** For example, as the boatswain tries to keep the ship afloat, the pair throw slurs and insults, with Antonio's exclamation "hang cur, hang you whoreson insolent noise-maker!" being a particular stand-out.

Maliciousness: having ill-will, and intending to do harm to others.

The people on the boat become progressively more terrified until finally the ship goes down – very Titanic-esque except (unfortunately) without the lifeboats or Leonardo DiCaprio. Shame.

Act 1 Scene 2

And in a brilliant contrast to the first scene, this one is an absolute *shocker* in terms of length, so my official recommendation is to go grab a coffee or something before reading on!

The scene opens with Miranda and Prospero and we're immediately told it was in fact Prospero who caused the storm. Miranda **laments** as an audience member, just like us, articulating how we felt watching the opening scene: "O, I have suffered / With those that I saw suffer: a brave vessel, / Who had, no doubt, some noble creature in her / Dashed all to pieces." This alerts us to the question that Shakespeare wants the audience to wrestle with for the entirety of the play – are Prospero's actions done in the name of good, or are they just plain evil? If Miranda finds them disturbing, shouldn't we think so too?

Lament: to express passionate grief or sorrow.

Prospero takes off his magical coat (which could perhaps be **symbolic** of him shedding the illusion about his past) and finally decides it's time to tell her their backstory. Miranda responds with the Shakespearean version of "about time, don't you think Dad?" He reveals (rather dramatically) that "thy father was the Duke of Milan and / A prince of power," before launching into his sob story of a past.

He tells Miranda that while he was the Duke of Milan, he spent so much time reading (same, Prospero, same) that he left governing to his evil brother, Antonio. Eventually, Antonio became so powerful that "he did believe / He was indeed the duke" and sought to overthrow his own brother. Prospero continues his really long story, explaining that Antonio achieved this by conning Alonso, the King of Naples, into backing him with a pretty dodgy financial deal. Antonio and his conspirators then shipped Prospero and Miranda away on an even dodgier boat. Great brother, huh?

Luckily, the two were able to survive thanks to good old Gonzalo, "a noble Neapolitan" who not only gave them food and water, but also "of his gentleness, / Knowing I [Prospero] loved my books, he furnished me / From mine own library with volumes that / I prize above my dukedom." This is a really interesting piece of dialogue, as it contrasts Gonzalo and his **good nature** with Antonio and his **evil nature**. It makes Antonio's actions seem all the more awful as we now have an **extreme point of comparison to hold him accountable to.** This contrast between characters is called a **foil**.

Foil: the use of two characters to highlight their distinct qualities.

Shakespeare uses foils throughout *The Tempest* to raise important questions about morality/immorality and the uses/abuses of power. It's all about using **duality** to make a point.

Even though Miranda has been brought up to date with all that super important info, she's still unsure why her father actually caused the shipwreck (she doesn't yet know who is on the boat!). Prospero tells her that "bountiful Fortune, / Now my dear lady, hath mine enemies / Brought to this shore" and that now is the time to make them pay, as he might never get the chance again. This exchange foregrounds that revenge is going to be a really significant theme in the play which will bring up heaps of questions about morality, time, and the difference between right and wrong. It's important to note that Prospero seems *pretty* committed to revenge at this point in the play, which makes his decision to later forgive the usurpers all the more interesting. From this point forward, I want you to really pay attention to the changes in his attitude so that we can develop a sophisticated analysis of Prospero as a character!

Prospero gets pretty sick of Miranda's questions, so he casts a spell on her and sends her to sleep. I mean, this is a pretty big power move and it doesn't reflect well on Prospero. Not only has he at this point in the text consistently interrupted his story to tell Miranda to obey him and listen, **he's actually interfered with her personal autonomy.** While this kind of familial dynamic was kind of the norm at the time (not the magic part, but the whole patriarchal thing) it definitely doesn't sit right with most modern audiences and their relationship is thus a great discussion point in modern analyses.

Moving from one messed up power dynamic to another, Prospero calls his fairy servant, Ariel, to him and asks for a report on the tempest that they created together. The sheer terror that the courtiers must have experienced is revealed to the audience through Ariel's descriptive, visually magnificent dialogue: "sometime I'd divide, / And burn in many places. On the topmast, / The yards, and bowspirit would I flame distinctly, / Then meet and join." This imagery of **fiery horror** signals to the audience that this island is a treacherous wild place in which some serious **moral forces** are at work. **Fire is symbolic of things like destruction, renewal, and damnation,** so it's no surprise Shakespeare has used it to introduce the courtiers to the island. We're also told that apparently Ferdinand was *so* terrified by the whole ordeal that he shouted "Hell is empty, and all the devils are here!" Just like the fire symbolism, we're getting pretty strong indications from this line that the island is a place of damnation in which people have to come face to face with their sins.

After telling Prospero about all the ways in which Ariel met his master's demands (including making sure that all of the courtiers were brought to shore without being harmed), Ariel starts to get a little "moody." He argues that he's worked super hard for Prospero and now it's time for Prospero to give Ariel his "liberty" Ariel goes on a bit of a rant: "remember I have done thee worthy service, / Told thee no lies, made no mistakings, served / Without or grudge or grunblings." And here's where Prospero's true character comes out. Rather than thanking Ariel for his service, he instead manipulates him by asking "dost thou forget / From what a torment I did free thee?"

The "torment" he's referring to is the former master of the island, "the foul witch Sycorax." Sycorax was this mean old witch (according to Prospero) who Ariel used to serve. She's also the mother of Caliban but we'll get to that in a minute! Since Ariel was "a spirit too delicate / To act her earthy and abhorred command," she imprisoned him in a tree which Prospero then saved him from when he rocked up on the island. Prospero's use of this memory is pretty cruel, especially as he uses it to threaten Ariel into obeying him or else he will "rend an oak / And peg thee in his knotty entrails till / Thou hast howled away twelve winters."

Prospero's use of rhetoric here is really interesting as it shows he's gotten pretty good at controlling others through language, and magic for that matter. He constantly uses Ariel's past to blackmail him into further work, but also **to legitimate Prospero's power on the island.** If Prospero hadn't saved Ariel, do you think he would still have the same kind of control of the island? Prospero's whole schtick is presenting himself as the moral force for good and other opponents for power as evil (as we saw just as a moment ago when he told Miranda all about how he was usurped).

It's important to explore how **Prospero uses language to manipulate the past, others, and emotions in his favour,** so definitely keep an eye out for it as you read through the text.

Prospero, having consolidated his control, then sends Ariel off on a new mission – Ariel must make himself "a nymph o'th'sea; / Be subject to no sight but thine and mine, invisible / To every eyeball else." Having sent Ariel on his way, he awakens Miranda and tells her that they are going to visit Caliban, who Prospero refers to as "my slave." Miranda, who has so far been characterised as kind and good, joins in on the Caliban hate, saying, "Tis a villain, sir, / I do not love to look on." Before even seeing Caliban, the audience is given a pretty poor impression of him. First, we're told that he's the son of the evil Sycorax, and now Miranda (who is characterised as kind and innocent) is hating on him. This is important given that Caliban is in fact the actual true master of the island, not Prospero, because of his heritage. It begins the play's complex relationship with colonialism and power and will only continue to get more intense.

Caliban enters and immediately reinforces the negative things we've heard about him so far. He hurls curse after curse at Prospero and Miranda, yelling things like "as wicked dew as e'er my mother brushed / With raven's feather from unwholesome fen / Drop on you both!" Prospero's response is important here, as it shows the absolute, and perhaps cruel, power that he is able to wield over Caliban. He immediately retorts "for this, be sure, tonight thou shalt bave cramps, / Side-stiches, that shall pen thy breath up; urchins / Shall, for that vast of night that they may work, / All exercise on thee." This kind of intimidation reveals the sheer **physical and brutal power** Prospero has over everyone on the island, and slightly unnerves the audience. Prospero is kind of set up as the good guy (seeing as he was unfairly usurped and all by his own brother) but this abuse of power seems a little extreme. Just like in Prospero's interactions with Miranda and Ariel, Shakespeare embeds **moral questions** within the Prospero-Caliban dynamic. Is Prospero a fair and just master? Especially when we consider the fact that the island isn't really his?

The power dynamics of colonialism really come into play here, with Caliban recounting how Prospero and Miranda at first treated him well but then quickly turned him into a slave. He argues, "this Island's mine, by Sycorax my mother, / Which thou tak'st from me" before launching into a pitiful monologue about how initially Prospero and Ariel had "strok'st me, and made much of me" and in turn, Caliban had "loved thee, / And showed thee all the qualities o'th'isle." But the moment Prospero had taken control, he quickly disregarded Caliban and made him his slave.

An interesting point about colonialism and Westernisation comes through in this monologue – Caliban tells us that the two had taught him how "to name the bigger light," which is Shakespearean for "sun." The teaching of English to colonised peoples has long been a complex part of Western expansionism and is often used as an argument for colonisation as many believe it to be a civilised and modern language. But this inherently **has colonial and racist implications** because if English is civilised and good, what does that make Caliban's previous language? Was Caliban uncivilised just because he didn't **espouse** Western traditions?

Espouse: to advocate or support something.

The exchange between Caliban, Prospero, and Miranda just gets more and more tense, with Prospero accusing Caliban of violating "the honour of my child." Caliban then responds that if Prospero hadn't stopped him, he would have "peopled else / This isle with Calibans." This has a few potential meanings, but many read this as an accusation that Caliban had actually tried to rape Miranda but Prospero had stopped him before he could "populate" the island with their children. Miranda is hurt by this and really takes it out on Caliban, calling him an "abhorrèd slave." When Caliban then tries to have a go at Miranda, Prospero interferes and calls him a "hag-seed," which means child of a hag/witch. It's a pretty hefty insult and he follows it up with a series of threats. Caliban recognises that there's no way out of this and admits that he "must obey" Prospero's demands that he fetch wood for them.

Believe it or not, this scene *still* isn't over, because here comes the music! Caliban leaves to fetch wood, and Ariel enters singing a beautiful song with Ferdinand in tow. Many scholars tend to overlook the importance of music in this play, but it is in fact a vital element of the text as a whole. The music in *The Tempest* is often used to further **disorient and unsettle the courtiers** who are desperately trying to find some sense of sanity on the island.

In case you need a quick reminder, Ferdinand is the King of Naples' son and was one of the courtiers who went down on the ship. Ariel, however, ensured he made it safely to shore but away from the others, all to play into Prospero's grand plan for revenge. This is the first time we've seen the courtiers since the whole Titanic drama, so a little bit of **exposition** is provided – Ferdinand believes his father is drowned. But what's even more important than the exposition is the fact that we are now introduced to the sheer magic and awe of the island through his eyes: "sitting on a bank, / Weeping again the King my father's wreck, / This music crept by me upon the waters, / Allaying both their fury and my passion / With its sweet air."

Exposition: a literary device which provides a bit of description or explanation.

Prospero points out Ferdinand to Miranda and being *literally* the first human she's ever seen apart from her father, she at first believes he's a spirit, exclaiming, "Lord, how it looks about! Believe me, sir, / It carries a brave form. But 'tis a spirit," who we know is Miranda. After realising that Ferdinand is in fact a man, she falls instantly in love with him. Ferdinand, in awe of finding a chick on the island, let alone such a magical one, also falls in love, quickly proclaiming that he'll make her the Queen of Naples. (Everyone always talks about how foolish Romeo and Juliet were for falling in love so quickly, but Ferdinand and Miranda are next level.)

Prospero is pleased with this turn of events, as it **all fits into his grand plan to regain power,** but he doesn't want them to get too ahead of themselves, so he picks a fight with Ferdinand (which he'll clearly win, given the magic powers and all!). He also lies to Miranda, seriously downplaying Ferdinand's value, proclaiming that "to th'most of men this is a Caliban, / And they to him are angels." Having slowed down their relationship just a little, Prospero beckons everyone off stage, finally ending this ridiculously long scene.

> **Ambiguity:** the quality of having no set-in-stone interpretation.

The most pertinent parts of this scene is the **ambiguity.** Prospero's use of power, for example, is never clearly endorsed or condemned by Shakespeare. Instead, it's up to the audience to decide how they feel about it. **constructed around Prospero's use of power and control.** In this scene alone, we see him abuse his power over Miranda, Ariel, Caliban, *and* Ferdinand. In each of these relationships, he uses language to coerce them into obeying his wishes and orders. **Prospero uses speech and history to cultivate his power, twisting the past and words to suit himself and his needs.** He also places a great deal of rhetorical emphasis on his good deeds and the bad deeds of others in order to position him as the morally superior individual, thereby **legitimating his control**. While Prospero is the 'good guy' to some, and perhaps in some ways serves as a voice for Shakespeare himself, this abuse of power (through lying, manipulation, curses, and intimidation) is alarming and suggests to the audience that Prospero's morality is a little more ambiguous than we might think.

Act 2 Scene 1

Alright, it's time to get acquainted with the Royal Squad! The important characters here are **Alonso, Gonzalo, Antonio,** and **Sebastian.** The gist of this scene is that the courtiers are drastically lost on the island, King Alonso is devastated over losing Ferdinand (oh, the **dramatic irony**!), and Gonzalo is trying, but failing, the cheer the poor man up.

Being the eternal optimist, Gonzalo tries to lighten the mood by arguing that "our hint of woe / Is common; every day some sailor's wife, / The masters of some merchant, and the merchant / Have just our theme of woe. But for the miracle, / I mean our preservation, few in millions / Can speak like us." But comparing the shipwreck to a miracle doesn't work, so he moves on to his next tactic – trying to convince everyone just how *beautiful* the island is. He seems to be seeing things very differently to the rest of the courtiers, especially Sebastian and Antonio who are determined to **heckle** the poor man the entire journey.

For example, Gonzalo exclaims "how lush and lusty the grass looks! How green!" and Antonio responds "the ground, indeed, is **tawny**." This **contrast in the perception of the island** is *pretty* important for two reasons. Firstly, it reveals the poor nature of Sebastian and Antonio compared to Gonzalo. Their constant heckling is awful, especially given Gonzalo's optimism and kind nature. It also sets them up as morally bankrupt, which means their later betrayal is framed negatively in the audience's mind. But secondly, and perhaps most significantly, **the contrasting perspectives of the island helps to construct the island in the audiences' minds.** Staging a play realistically in the Elizabethan theatre was pretty hard, so Shakespeare uses the language of the characters to show the audience what the island could look like. Plus, **the multiplicity of perspectives further enriches the mysticism and disorienting nature of the island.**

Gonzalo continues to be amazed by the island and tries to get Alonso in on the positivity. He is shocked "that our garments, being, as they were, drenched in the sea, hold notwithstanding their freshness and gloss, being rather new-dyed than stained with salt water." Alonso doesn't seem to be listening, so he tries to include Alonso in the story but Alonso goes off. He retorts with a **synecdoche** where he uses "ears" to refer to him more generally. It creates a more specific, and therefore more significant image for the audience to grapple with. In this instance, it enables us to better understand how Alonso's grief is affecting him. His sheer emotional turmoil over losing his son on the journey back from his daughter's marriage is evident in his exclamation that "you cram these words into mine ears against / The stomach of my sense." Furthermore, he laments "would I had never married my daughter there! For, coming thence, / My son is lost, and, in my rate, she too."

Dramatic irony: a literary device in which the audience understands the situation better than the actual characters on stage. For example, King Alonso laments the loss of his son, but the audience is aware that Ferdinand is alive, having just seen him on stage lamenting the loss of his father!

Heckle: to interrupt with derisive, sarcastic, or aggressive comments.

Tawny: a orange-brown colour.

Synecdoche: a literary device in which a part is used to symbolise the whole.

Sebastian, failing to read the room, turns on Alonso and blames *him* for the loss of their heir. He argues, "sir, you may thank yourself for this great loss, / That would not bless our Europe with your daughter, / But rather loose her to an African." This cruel argument has **deeply racist connotations,** as Sebastian is condemning marrying Alonso's daughter to person of colour. Gonzalo tries to stand up for the poor grieving king, telling Sebastian "you rub the sore, / When you should bring the plaster."

Utopian: refers to something that is ideal or perfect.

When that fails to relieve the tension, Gonzalo launches into a monologue in which he fantasises about what his utopian society on the island would look like. He proclaims that on *his* island, there'd be no leader and not a single man would have to work: "no occupation, all men idle, all." It becomes clear that **he values purity and equality, things which stand in clear contrast with the power politics played by most of the characters in the play.** While his ideals are clearly just ideals, especially with the amount of heckling he receives, it's clear that Shakespeare's positive portrayal of Gonzalo endorses his version of politics over the scheming and power politics of the other characters.

Soon after he finishes his monologue, Ariel enters and begins to play music, sending Gonzalo and Alonso to sleep. Now that the king and his trusty advisor are asleep, it's time for some *serious* plotting. Antonio and Sebastian are unaffected by the music and are clearly shocked by the sudden sleepiness of the other courtiers: "they fell together all, as by consent; / They dropped, as by a thunderstroke."

Left to his own devices, Antonio begins to plot once more. It's clear that **he's incredibly power hungry** given his history of usurpation, but now it's happening right out in the open in front of the audience. He hints to Sebastian that now both of Alonso's heirs are gone, Sebastian himself could become the King of Naples: 'My strong imagination sees a crown / Dropping upon thy head.' This synecdoche has a powerful effect on the audience as it **enables them to envision the corrupt transfer of power** that could take place if Alonso is killed. When Sebastian protests that Claribel is still alive, Antonio argues that there's so much space between Claribel and Naples, "a space whose every cubit / Seems to cry out, 'How shall that Claribel / Measure us back to Naples? Keep in Tunis, / And let Sebastian wake'." Finally Sebastian succumbs to Antonio's power politics, declaring "as thou got'st Milan, I'll come by Naples."

Suddenly, Ariel plays some more music and the courtiers wake up to Antonio and Sebastian preparing to kill the king. The scheming pair bumble to cover up their tracks, Sebastian blaming their drawn swords on the fact that they "heard a hollow burst of bellowing / Like bulls, or rather lions." Antonio gets in on the lie, confirming that "sure it was the roar / Of a whole herd of lions." The courtiers decide to exit the stage (given the lions and all) in the hopes of finding Alonso's son, Ferdinand.

This scene is really important as it **helps us understand the power politics that dominated Europe at the time.** In his **characterisation** of Antonio and Sebastian, Shakespeare condemns this form of politics and **foreshadows the demise that the courtiers will experience because of their moral corruption.**

> **Characterisation:** the way an author portrays their characters with specific qualities.

Act 2 Scene 2

After what has been a pretty tragic start to a play defined as a comedy, it's *finally* time for some comedic relief. But keep in mind as we go through this analysis that the scene's humour doesn't inherently negate its meaning or importance. It actually deals with some of the main messages of the play in a much more nuanced way than the more serious scenes!

The scene opens with Caliban lugging some wood around the stage, cursing his master: "all the infections that the sun sucks up / From bogs, fens, flats, on Prosper fall, and make him / By inch-meal a disease!" While Caliban rants against his master, Trinculo (Alonso's jester) enters, dazed and confused. Caliban, having only met the people on the island, **fears Trinculo is a spirit coming to punish him for his disobedience.** He quickly ducks for cover, only for Trinculo to stumble over him, believing him either 'A man or a fish'. There's a clap of thunder and Trinculo ducks for cover with Caliban.

To further the comedy of the scene, a very drunk Stephano (Alonso's butler) then enters singing a banger of a tune. He stumbles across Stephano and Caliban's pile of limbs and believes it a 'monster of the isle with four legs.' He then, however, hears Trinculo's voice and drags him out from the cover. The pair offer Caliban alcohol, which quickly enchants him and casts him under their spell. Caliban proclaims "that's a brave god, and bears celestial liquor. I will kneel to him."

However funny this drunken Caliban is, we must pay attention to the **parallels.** When Prospero and Miranda came to the island all that time ago, Caliban quickly accepted Prospero as his master. Now, the moment Trinculo and Stephano give him a little bit of alcohol, he discards his old master to obey their words. He proclaims that he'll "show thee every fertile inch o'th'island, and I will kiss thy foot. I prithee, be my god." The process seems to be **mirroring the colonisation process** Caliban has already gone through once; even though Stephano and Trinculo treat him terribly, repeatedly calling him "monster," **Caliban is willing to give up his home for a small gain.**

Some more music plays and off the comedic foils go, with the "brave monster" leading the way.

Act 3 Scene 3

For a bit of a change of pace, we now have a cute little romantic scene to enjoy! Ferdinand enters, as the stage directions highlight, "bearing a log." He's been tasked with doing Prospero's dirty work, but he's taking it like a champ. As he works, he muses about Miranda, enjoying his work because she "makes my labours pleasures." Cute!

Miranda enters, with Prospero in tow but out of their sight. Believing her father is "hard at study," she beckons him to rest and spend some time with her. She reveals her sheer love for him, promising "if you'll sit down, / I'll bear your logs the while." Ferdinand one-ups this demonstration of love, using language that underscores his **obstinacy:** "no precious creature, / I had rather crack my sinews, break my back, / Than you should such dishonour undergo / While I sit lazy by."

Obstinacy: being stubborn and difficult.

Lavish: over-the-top or elaborate.

While these **lavish** exchanges of love unfold, Prospero watches on and refers to his daughter as a "poor worm" who is "infected!" The lovey-dovey stuff doesn't end there though, because the pair continues to heap on the romance until eventually **Miranda straight up asks him to marry her** (way to subvert gender norms, sister!) As the happily engaged pair trot off, Prospero declares how happy *he* is, for everything is falling into place.

While this scene is clearly all about romance, it again sparks some interesting questions about power and control. The scene begins with Ferdinand clearly a slave to Prospero's commands, but when Miranda enters, he quickly becomes a servant to her love, as is she. She explains to him that even if he chooses not to marry her, she'll "be your servant / Whether you will or no." **This reveals some pretty alarming gender dynamics** – Miranda has grown pretty used to being subjected to the will of the men around her. She grew up under Prospero's command, and now, she's promised to be a servant to the first man she's *ever* met other than her own father... this inevitably engenders the audience's concerns about whether **love and relationships are forms of servitude,** just like the slavery that Caliban and Ariel have been subjected to on the island.

Act 3 Scene 2

The comedic trio is back and drunker than before! Trinculo and Stephano now refer to Caliban as their "servant monster" and order him around, but he seems reasonably happy to oblige. Plus, Stephano has assumed the position of power over the other two, **declaring himself the new master of the island.**

After a bit of back and forth, Caliban launches into his back story, just as Ariel enters the stage. Caliban tells the pair that he is "subject to a tyrant, a sorcerer, that by his cunning hath cheated me of the island." Ariel becomes enraged and shouts, "thou liest," but since he's invisible to those on stage, Caliban thinks Trinculo is the one who says it. A fight ensues, as Ariel encourages them, and it takes Stephano shutting Trinculo down to bring an end to the antagonism. Stephano's role as the more powerful one in the trio is really interesting because it shows the process of **domination and control unfold in a comedic setting,** allowing for Shakespeare's more nuanced critique of power in general.

Caliban then launches into a murderous rant, listing all the ways they could kill Prospero: "there thou mayst brain him, / Having first seized his books; or with a log / Batter his skull, or paunch him with a stake, / Or cut his weasand with thy knife." Stephano and Trinculo are convinced by Caliban to kill Prospero for two reasons: firstly, if Prospero is dead then Stephano can be the true ruler of the island, and secondly, Caliban promises that Stephano will be able to marry Miranda, who he describes as a "**nonpareil**."

Nonpareil: unrivalled, or having no equal.

This is a really interesting plot development, as it sets Stephano and Trinculo up as **analogues** to Antonio and Sebastian. Both pairs are usurpers, desperate to take as much power as possible. Even though Stephano and Trinculo are comedic characters, their manipulation of Caliban for their own personal gain and plan to overthrow Prospero is as important a critique of power politics and moral corruption as Antonio and Sebastian's plotline.

Analogues: a person or thing that can be compared to another as a parallel.

Ariel, still watching on, begins to play some music which causes Trinculo and Stephano to absolutely freak out. But Caliban, being used to the island and all of its magic, calms them down. Caliban's following monologue is honestly my favourite part of the entire play and deserves an entire book of its own analysis, but I'll condense it down for you.

In response to the music, Caliban urges them to "be not afeard; this isle is full of noises, / Sounds, and sweet airs, that give delight and hurt not. Sometimes a thousand twangling instruments will hum about mine ears; and sometimes voices." He continues to discuss the beauty of the environment, revealing to the audience **his true and deep connection with the island.** His lyrical language, full of auditory imagery, is a testament to the fact that the island to be his and his alone, **allowing him a few seconds of ownership and freedom.**

The sheer beauty of this speech encourages the audience to feel empathy for a character who has been consistently portrayed as a monster (I'm not crying, you're crying!). In doing so, Shakespeare **invites us into a criticism of the people and processes which have taken the island away from Caliban.** In a postcolonial reading of *The Tempest,* these powers are interpreted as the dynamics of colonialism and thus the empathy we feel for Caliban enable a criticism of Western colonisation.

Act 3 Scene 3

It's now time to turn our attention back to the courtiers who are unfortunately still lost on the island. The maze of an island has absolutely worn the 'Royal Squad' out – poor Gonzalo's bones are aching, and Alonso is completely down in the dumps. Antonio is "right glad that he's [Alonso's] so out of hope" because it means he and Sebastian can follow through on their plot to take the throne for themselves. Just as the sneaky duo agree to kill Alonso tonight, **portentous** music begins to play... which we know means something's up! Spirits enter, bringing a whole banquet with them before promptly exiting.

Portentous: something ominous that foreshadows what is to come.

Having spent the past few hours stumbling around the island, this is the last straw for the courtiers! They are *completely* overwhelmed by the display, with Sebastian delivering possibly the best line in the entire play: **"Now I will believe / That there are unicorns."** Gonzalo is also blown away by the entire ordeal, asking "if in Naples / I should report this now, would they believe me?" He then delivers a pretty sick burn, remarking that these spirits in fact have more manners than most of humanity. This play has a lot to say about immorality and evil, but Gonzalo sums it up so succinctly – if spirits, *literal spirits*, have a better nature than humans, what does that say about us?

Harpy: a mythological creature that is a human-bird hybrid.

Just as Alonso goes to eat the banquet, Ariel enters dressed like a **harpy** and delivers one of the most terrifying monologues ever written! What follows is an analysis of some of the most important themes and language features of this speech.

Censure: a condemnation or rejection of something.

The whole thing begins with a **censure** of Alonso, Antonio, and Sebastian: "you are three men of sin, whom destiny, / That hath to instrument this lower world / And what is in't, the never-surfeited sea / Hath caused to belch up you." Note here that Ariel says *three* men of sin and not *four* men of sin. He deliberately excludes Gonzalo from the criticism, because this speech is part of Prospero's plan for revenge, designed to intimidate the hell out of the three men and break *their* spirits, not Gonzalo's.

Ariel creates a terrifying barrage of words with which the three men must grapple, jumping from lines such as "I have made you mad" to an outright recounting of their sins: "but remember – / For that's my business to you – that you three / From Milan did supplant good Prospero." All of this would have been pretty alarming to the courtiers, given that they've washed up on an island in the middle of nowhere. They have absolutely no idea that this is Prospero's island, so to them, Ariel is a spirit who is condemning their past sins, rather than Prospero's servant exacting revenge. To Shakespeare's contextual audience, this would have really resonated given the pervasive influence of religious understandings of morality at the time. They would have recognised how terrifying this speech would have been for the courtiers given their belief in the religious need for **absolution.** to come to terms with sin.

Absolution: coming to terms with one's sin, and seeking forgiveness.

The exorbitant impact this speech has on the courtiers is clearly demonstrated in Alonso's response. He laments, "O, it is monstrous, monstrous!" before recounting the shock he felt at hearing Prospero's name on such an island. At this point, Alonso feels so horrible about his past sins that he delivers a devastating few lines: "therefore my son i' th' oozde is bedded, and / I'll seek him deeper than e'er plummet sounded, / And with him there lie mudded." Gonzalo wraps up the scene by recognising the effect that the three men's sins are having on them. Shakespeare uses his simile "their great guilt, / Like poison given to work a great time after, / Now 'gins to bite the spirits," to **intimate** to the audience the sheer consequences of sin and immorality.

Intimate: to convey or suggest.

While this whole scene can seem quite **didactic,** it is not uncommon for Shakespeare's works to have moral implications from which the audience can learn. Upon first glance, this scene appears to be an ostensible condemnation of sin and exacting of justice, yet a deeper reading can uncover a different meaning. While Ariel can be viewed as the **exacter of justice** who is able to rightfully punish the three courtiers, a closer analysis reveals that perhaps **he is simply Prospero's mouthpiece, only reciting the lines he's been taught to say rather than authentically bringing about justice.** In this vein, the whole scene actually reveals Prospero's sheer amount of power and manipulation once again. The devastating effect the harpy speech has on the courtiers is quite apparent – Alonso is even considering killing himself – encouraging the audience to reconsider Prospero's status as a hero. Is Prospero the evil one here, given his awful manipulation of everyone's emotions and lives (not just of the courtiers, but everyone else on the island too)?

Didactic: designed to teach or provide moral instruction.

Act 4 Scene 1

Time for a bit of a mood change, as this scene's all about Ferdinand and Miranda's marriage! Marriage is a pretty important theme in Shakespeare's plays, **often symbolising unity, harmony, and resolution.** But in *The Tempest,* this marriage couldn't be further from resolution, as it's all part of Prospero's plan to exact some serious revenge against his usurpers and regain power.

The scene opens with a somewhat shocking discussion about Miranda's virginity – Prospero warns Ferdinand that he shouldn't "break her virgin-knot before / All sanctimonious ceremonies may / With full and holy rite be ministered." Ferdinand promises he won't, so having sorted that drama out, Prospero orders some spirits to perform a **masque** for the two lovers.

Three spirits, modelled on the mythological goddesses **Iris, Juno, and Ceres** appear and bless the happy couple one by one. The use of a masque here is pretty interesting, especially as it highlights important traditional perceptions of marriage and family life. **Masques were common forms of entertainment in Shakespeare's time**, involving masked actors acting out well known stories. Ferdinand is in complete awe, declaring "this is a most majestic vision, and / Harmonious charmingly." He loves it so much he begs, "let me live here ever! So rare a wondered father and a wife / Makes this place paradise."

> **Aside:** a theatrical device where a character is heard only by the audience and not by the other characters on stage. This is often used to heighten tension, or create dramatic irony.

But before we can get too carried away with a happy ending, Prospero remembers Caliban's plan and delivers an excellent **aside:** "I had forgot that foul conspiracy / Of the beast Caliban and his confederates / Against my life." He explains to the couple that "our revels now are ended," before launching into some musings about the meaning of life, delivering the poignant line "we are such stuff / As dreams are made on, and our little life / Is rounded with a sleep." This monologue is really important because **it seems Prospero is committing to his seeing his plan through to the end.** Many people view Prospero as representative of Shakespeare, so to some, these lines represent Shakespeare gearing up to give up his pen and see out the end of his career.

Prospero then calls Ariel to him, preparing to meet with Caliban. They decide to hang some beautiful clothes on a line at Prospero's house, aiming to lure the three usurpers into stealing the fine clothing so they can catch them. With Prospero and Ariel still present, Caliban, Stephano, and Trinculo enter drunk and wet. Upon seeing the clothes, Stephano and Trinculo decide to steal them, whereas Caliban urges them to just get the murder done: "let't alone / And do the murder first. If he awake, / From toe to crown he'll fill our skins with pinches, / Make us strange stuff."

Their attempts to overthrow Prospero are portrayed as hilarious, and even humiliating. They can't stay focused for long enough to even follow through on their plans. After dressing themselves in the fine clothing, Prospero sets a pack of spirits disguised as hounds on the trio, scaring them off. Having just evoked empathy from the audience by being vulnerable about his age and life, Prospero has a few extra brownie points compared to Caliban, who is drawing less and less empathy from the audience given his whole murderous plot. At this point, the audience is forced to come to terms with who, and what, they support going into the final act. Whose position is more understandable or honourable? Prospero's? Or Caliban's?

Act 5 Scene 1

The time has come for Prospero to exact the final part of his revenge plot – **confrontation!**

The scene begins with Ariel reporting on the state of the courtiers, telling Prospero that they are "brimful of sorrow and dismay." He also tells Prospero, however, that he has made poor old Gonzalo cry: "his tears run down his beard like winter's drops / From eaves of reeds." This line is heartbreaking, **revealing the devastating impact that Prospero has had not just on his enemies, but on the people he loves.** It furthers the audience's questioning of the morality and ethics of Prospero's actions – if he's made his old friend Gonzalo cry, is his desire for revenge that worthy of respect?

Gonzalo's tears are *so* devastating that even Prospero considers the ethics of his revenge plot. He completely changes his mind, sending Ariel to fetch the courtiers and bring them to him. This change of heart is incredibly interesting and raises lots of questions – was it Gonzalo's emotions alone which changed his mind or is something else at play? Perhaps it was Ariel's remark that, **if Ariel were human, he would feel sad about the mental state of the courtiers** that set Prospero off. If even a spirit can feel more empathy for the courtiers than Prospero, perhaps that's a sign that Prospero needs to reconsider the role that magic and control has in his life.

Prospero announces that his time has come and he must finally give up his magic by breaking his staff and drowning his book. He reminisces on his relationship with magic throughout the past few years, allowing the audience into his world. Prospero's ethics, however, come seriously into question when he announces that he has abused his magic so extremely, even having raised the dead: "graves at my command / Have waked their sleepers, oped and let 'em forth / By my so potent art." In Shakespeare's time, **necromancy** was considered a seriously evil thing, so for his contextual audience, **this admission would surely have had a great effect on the way they viewed Prospero.**

Necromancy: 'black magic,' or sorcery associated with raising the dead.

Halfway through his monologue, Ariel enters bringing with him the Royal Squad! They are lured into Prospero's magic circle, "and there stand charmed." Prospero then talks to them one-by-one, encouraging the audience to see these characters the way he sees them. He approaches Gonzalo first, and gets all emotional, thanking him for being an "honourable man." He promises, "I will pay thy graces / Home both in word and deed."

He then moves on to Alonso and the tone *really* changes. Alonso's guilt has slowly been unravelled throughout the play, culminating in this moment of confrontation. While Alonso is charmed and can't really respond, **Prospero's condemnation of Alonso in front of the audience is clearly Prospero's way of getting justice without needing to exact cruel revenge.** He chides Sebastian's acts as well, before moving on to the big one: his confrontation with his own brother, Antonio. His condemnation of Antonio's actions, which include plotting to kill his own king, is enough for Prospero, because rather than harming him, he admits, "I do forgive thee, / Unnatural though thou art."

Ariel sings another cute little song, while dressing Prospero in his magical garments. Prospero, remembering his promise to free Ariel, acknowledges that "I shall miss / Thee, but yet thou shalt have freedom." Ariel departs on another mission, just as the courtiers come to their senses. Gonzalo cries out, "all torment, trouble, wonder, and amazement / Inhabits here." Remember, they all still have *no idea* that this is Prospero's island, and after the absolute hell they've been through in the past few hours, this whole scenario must seem like some strange hallucination.

Prospero assures the courtiers that it is indeed him, "the wronged Duke of Milan, Prospero" and Alonso is so gobsmacked that he can't apologise quick enough. Alonso instantly strips Antonio of his dukedom and returns it to Prospero, begging him for forgiveness. Prospero then has a cute little reunion with Gonzalo, giving his old friend a big embrace.

But cue the dramatic music, because before we can get all caught up in the good vibes, Prospero turns on Sebastian and Antonio. He warns them that he could say all sorts of things which would get them in trouble (like, he could literally tell Alonso about their assassination plot) but refrains, because apparently Prospero's a good guy now. Sebastian exclaims "the devil speaks in him!" to which Prospero straight up responds, "no," before he rounds on his brother Antonio. **Prospero forgives his brother, showing some pretty significant character growth here, having gone from a revenge-driven, salty old man to someone willing to show forgiveness to those who wronged him.**

Before Antonio can respond, Alonso cuts in and tells Prospero that he has lost, "my dear son Ferdinand." Alonso is clearly pretty devastated by the whole ordeal, arguing, "irreparable is the loss, and patience / Says it is past her cure." Rather than telling Alonso that his son is in fact alive, Prospero decides to be a bit cryptic. Prospero says that **he too has lost a child in this tempest,** which articulates the grief he feels about losing his daughter to marriage. Alonso delivers the excellently ironic line: "O heavens, that they were living both in Naples / The king and queen there!" This is pretty funny because the audience (and Prospero) knows that their two children are in fact married and living their best lives on the island.

Prospero decides to have a little more fun before revealing Ferdinand and Miranda playing chess in his cell. The choice of chess is pretty symbolic because, after all, chess is a game with kings and queens and knights all battling it out for victory... a clear parallel to the events that transpire in *The Tempest*.

Alonso, having been through a lot on this island, doesn't quite believe his eyes, sighing, "if this prove / A vision of the island, one dear son / Shall I twice lose." Ferdinand is also shocked, having believed his father drowned in the shipwreck. But arguably, the person most shocked by this whole ordeal is our girl Miranda, who is absolutely in awe of all of the men that stand before her. I mean, in one day she's gone from only knowing one man (her father), to marrying the only other guy she's ever met, to finding a whole bunch of courtiers in her watching her play chess. Big day, if you ask me.

Her **sheer naivety and innocence** really shines through in her reaction: "O wonder! / How many goodly creatures are there here ! / How beauteous mankind is! O brave new world. / That has such people in't!" Her amazement is kind of cute, but this is tempered when we remember that this **innocence has been imposed on her by her own father**... but more on that later.

Alonso brings up the elephant in the room, pointing out that Ferdinand can't have known Miranda for longer than three hours, but nevertheless, Ferdinand tells his dad that he's now got a daughter-in-law. To Alonso's credit, he doesn't react negatively, but rather, asks Miranda for forgiveness, given the whole exile of her and her father all those years ago. Gonzalo is absolutely overjoyed by this news, invoking the gods: "look down, you gods, / And on this couple drop a blessed crown!" **This signals a happy resolution,** demonstrating that the two warring families have finally come to peace with one another and thereby **symbolising Prospero's resolution with his past.**

Ariel then enters, bringing with him the Master and the Boatswain and more good news – the courtiers are told that everyone is alive and the ship "is tight and yare and bravely rigged as when / We first put out to sea," which essentially means it's good to go! Finally, everyone can get off this darned island!

But before everyone departs, Ariel brings in the final set of usurpers Prospero needs to reckon with: Caliban, Stephano, and Trrinculo. They've been on the run for a while at this point (remember how Prospero set a pack of spirits in the form of hounds on them?) and are still pretty drunk. While this is clearly a comedic moment – after all of their plans for revenge and usurpation, the three are clearly absolute messes – there's definitely an interesting moment between Caliban and Prospero. Prospero, referring to Calban, declares, "this thing of darkness I / acknowledge mine." This is a curious utterance from the master, who has so clearly condemned Caliban as being of the witch Sycorax, and stands in stark contrast to Prospero's prior dismissal of Caliban as a 'hag-seed." Is this an admission that **Prospero has played a role in making Caliban the dark twisted monster that he is?**

Alonso recognises his butler and jester and asks them how they came to be in such a pickle. Trinculo makes a good joke about pickles, being a jester and all, before the three of them are sent to clean up Prospero's cell if they want redemption.

Prospero and Caliban have an electrifying farewell, in which Caliban laments that he was a "thrice double ass" to "take this drunkard for a god, / And worship this dull fool!" While this is clearly about Stephano, it definitely has some important implications for Caliban's relationship with Prospero. If Caliban had such a strong and beautiful connection to his island, and is the clear master of the island being the native, was he also a fool for worshipping Prospero when he first came to the island?

After the comedic trio depart, Prospero invites the whole gang to his cell before they leave the island. He promises that he too will return to Milan after seeing his daughter and Ferdinand officially married in Naples. Prospero then commands Ariel to ensure that their trip to Italy is safe and fair, before finally releasing him from Prospero's command.

Prospero, finally alone on the stage, delivers the famous epilogue. He admits that his magic is finally gone: "now my charms are all o'erthrown, / And what strength I have's mine own, / Which is most faint." He continues, arguing that he has been imprisoned by the audience and he is their servant, just as Ariel and Caliban were his. He begs to be released from the audience's grasp by asking them to clap for him. He reminds the audience that they would want to be released from their crimes, so they too should "let your indulgence set me free."

This epilogue really speaks to the reading of *The Tempest* as Shakespeare's final farewell to the theatre. Prospero's begging for forgiveness for his crimes (the controlling and manipulation of the people around him) sounds like Shakespeare begging for forgiveness for the exact same thing – the controlling and manipulation of his audiences through language. Just as Prospero has used history, stories, and magic to encourage people to obey his will and emotions, so too has Shakespeare made a career of weaving tales and altering people's perceptions, albeit through the magic of the pen rather than the magic of the staff. In this vein, the epilogue can be considered a farewell to Shakespeare's writing career; a 'so long' to his use of magic to persuade his audiences, and a final, poignant relinquishing of his powers to compel us to feel all of the "tempestuous noise" of his characters' emotional journeys.

And that, my friends, is the end of *The Tempest!*

Section 4

Character Analysis

Prospero

So, Prospero is our main dude on the island, and a lot of the themes of the play stem from his journey and emotional life. In fact, he's *so* important to the play that many people wonder why Shakespeare didn't just call *The Tempest* 'Prospero' instead (as so many of Shakespeare's other plays are named after their protagonists – *Hamlet, Macbeth, King Lear,* etc.).

I think the most important thing that we need to consider about Prospero is the **tension that arises between perceptions of him as morally good and morally bereft.** He is indeed set up as an intrinsically 'good' character through his status as the protagonist of the play and his history, but his actions throughout the play suggest otherwise.

Firstly, we're told (by Prospero) that he had been dethroned by his evil and scheming brother. This inherently positions the audience to feel empathy for the poor man. Plus, we're told that when we first moved to the island, he was able to triumph over the island's predecessor, Sycorax, and her dark magic. Traditionally, in texts which involve a struggle between two magical forces, when one side triumphs over the other, their magic is confirmed as morally superior. So, within the first few scenes of the play, **the audience is forced to empathise with and align themselves alongside Prospero.**

But as the play continues, the water becomes a *little* murkier. It becomes clear that **Prospero has used language to present history, and therefore himself, in a way that legitimises his control.** On top of this, **he uses and abuses of magic not just towards his enemies, but also his loved ones,** which make his morality a little more ambiguous than the audience may initially believe. In this way, **Prospero drives a lot of the tension in the play**, with his actions evoking a range of reactions from sympathy to disgust.

Beyond this moral ambiguity, another thing we should consider is the way that Prospero slips into the role of director/playwright through his use of magic. From the very opening scene, **Prospero is the one calling the shots** – he is literally the driver of the action, using his magic and power to sap away at the free agency of the other characters, turning them into his puppets.

This dynamic leads us to **a potential reading of Prospero as a representation of Shakespeare himself.** Prospero uses the 'art' of magic to control and manipulate the emotions of others, just as Shakespeare uses the art of writing to control and manipulate the emotions of his audience. Just substitute Prospero's staff for a pen, and the parallels are pretty clear!

This interpretation is made all the clearer when we look at how the play ends – with Prospero renouncing his magic to return to a 'normal' life and let go of his obsessive passion, which has had detrimental impacts on his life. He begs the audience to release him from his role by applauding for him, a poignant request given **it was Shakespeare's final play**. Is this Shakespeare asking to be released from his duties through recognition and applause so that he can remove himself from art's grip?

And finally, let's look at **Prospero's internal struggle between revenge and forgiveness**. It is perhaps Prospero's most interesting quality that he consistently struggles between being a vengeful bastard and a fair, sappy, old man. It's hard to pinpoint exactly *why* he changes his mind about revenge... perhaps he was never going to *actually* hurt them and he only wanted to confuse and taunt them. Perhaps Prospero changed his mind upon hearing that his good friend Gonzalo had been hurt by Prospero's actions. Perhaps it was his realisation of mortality and loss now that Miranda's been married off. Perhaps it was Ariel suggesting that he'd have more emotion for Prospero's prisoners than Prospero if he were human...

I'll leave it up to you to decide!

Miranda

Being Prospero's daughter, Miranda is clearly an important part of the play. But her significance extends far beyond her familial role; she forces us to contemplate some pretty big questions.

Miranda's most prominent (and some would say most admirable) trait is **her ability to force the audience into seeing the beauty and wonder of life.** Not only does her name mean 'wonder' or 'admired,' but her sheer naivety and innocence mean that **everything she sees is a new and exciting experience, and therefore a new and exciting experience for the audience.** When she first meets Ferdinand, literally the first man she's ever met besides her father, she believes he's a spirit. Then, when she's told he's a human, she falls immediately in love with him, believing him the most marvellous thing she's ever seen. Her excessive joy later in the play, when she meets the rest of the courtiers, has a profound effect on the audience. Her seemingly excessive reaction at simply meeting a few crusty old men ("How beauteous mankind is! O brave new world. / That has such people in't") **encourages the audience to consider the extraordinary nature of humanity**, therefore leading us to the same discovery as Miranda. She certainly brings an element of hope and excitement to what would otherwise be quite a dark play.

But this innocence and naivety definitely has some negative connotations too. I mean, the only reason why she is so amazed by Ferdinand is because she's been deliberately kept in the dark by her father. He refused to tell her her own history, **proving the power language has over Miranda.** This power dynamic is reinforced throughout the play by Prospero's consistent sapping of her autonomy in order to suit his needs. He continuously tells her to obey and listen to his long story, sends her to sleep (and admits he knows she can't choose otherwise), chooses her husband for her, and uses her as a pawn in his plans for revenge... yikes.

All of this definitely encourages a feminist reading of Miranda, **allowing us to gage the potentially misogynistic and patriarchal dimensions of the text**. Besides the fact that she is the *only* female character in the show, she is manipulated and subjected to the control of at least three of the men on the island: first Prospero her father, Caliban in his attempt to rape her, and then Ferdinand. To further this reading, it's important that we look at how she is characterised. She's described by her own father as a "prize" (Act 1 Scene 2) and she is consistently portrayed as a beautiful young girl whose innocence is her value.

Ariel

Ariel too **functions as a reflection of Prospero's uses and abuses of power.** His magical powers enable him to serve as Prospero's mouthpiece – it is through him that Prospero's revenge and manipulation occurs. But to keep Ariel under his command to fulfil these goals, Prospero's legitimisation of power and ownership of the island comes into play, with Prospero rehashing the story of how he released Ariel all that time ago.

Ariel also raises interesting questions about **justice.** Firstly, he's used to exact Prospero's justice by terrifying and bewildering the usurpers on the island. But because of his sheer impact on the courtiers, we are encouraged to reconsider whether or not this attainment of revenge is fair. Plus, Ariel seems to show more emotion than some of the other characters in the play, further encouraging the audience into a reconsideration of whether justice is in fact an injustice in this case. If a spirit can feel more empathy than real humans, it makes the other characters' lack of emotions all the more dismal.

Caliban

Caliban is the rightful owner of the island and this provides the play with **a deeply troubling and political underbelly.**

Through a **postcolonial reading**, **Caliban's character is a door to the processes of colonisation in action in Shakespeare's time.** This begins in his first scene, in which he is literally referred to as a slave. But the postcolonial connotations extend beyond the literal here. Yes he's poorly treated by Prospero and yes he's had the island taken from him, but the colonial implications bleed through more sinisterly when we look at the way language operates in the play. For example, Caliban highlights that initially Prospero and Miranda's English lessons were valuable and beneficial, using **verse.** In Shakespeare's plays, verse is normally reserved for elite characters while prose (plain text) is reserved for the lower classes, so it's definitely interesting that Caliban occasionally speaks in verse! to elucidate the wonder that was present early in their relationship: "When thou cam'st first / Thou strok'st me, and made much of me; wouldst give me / Water with berries in't, and teach me how / To name the bigger light."

But it very quickly becomes clear that Prospero's acquisition of English is actually used to control him, rather than uplift him. This is evident in Miranda's manipulation of Caliban when he arcs up: "I pitied thee, / Took pains to make thee speak, taught thee each hour / One thing or other. When thou didst not, savage, / Know thine own meaning, but wouldst gabble like / A thing most brutish, I endowed thy purposes / With words that made them known."

This reveals Caliban's control at the hands of his learned language, but also the **"mission civilisatrice"** which was apparent in Shakespeare's context. The "mission civilisatrice," or 'civilising mission,' was a common justification for colonisation, as **it implied that through the spread of Westernisation (i.e. through English), Europeans could uplift the 'savages' of the Orient.** This civilising mission leads us to opportunities to reconsider the relationship between Prospero and Caliban. As Caliban can be read as symbolic of the victims of colonisation, **Prospero can therefore be read as a perpetrator of the civilising mission.** After all, he initially takes Caliban in and tries to educate him to fit in with the Western ideals, teaching him language and poetry. This is particularly clear in Shakespeare's choice to make Prospero speak in both prose and verse (which as aforementioned, is pretty symbolic!) Plus, Prospero acknowledges in the final scene that Caliban is, in a way, his responsibility: "This thing of darkness I / Acknowledge mine."

Postcolonialism: a theoretical framework through concerned with the enduring ramifications of colonisation. A postcolonial reading of the play is kind of like putting on a pair of tinted glasses which help us to see things differently.

Verse: this just means poetry, or speaking in meter.

The Orient: this is scholar Edward Said's term for the non-Western world. In Shakespeare's time, 'the Orient' was characterised by the West as an exotic, savage, and brutal place filled with people exactly like Caliban.

This dynamic perhaps explains why Prospero and Miranda are in fact so hurt by Caliban's curses and actions. If Prospero knows Caliban can't actually enact his curses, why then does Prospero react with anger to Caliban's curses and later usurpation attempt? Perhaps because Prospero had desired to turn Caliban into his Western 'unsavage' ideal, but has routinely failed? In this vein, Caliban's poetic speech about his island in Act 3 Scene 2 represents what Caliban *could* have been under Prospero's teaching, if he had been able to overcome his intrinsically 'savage' nature.

This postcolonial reading invites the audience into a reconsideration of Prospero's control of the island and Caliban. Even though Caliban is on a mission to usurp him, the audience is encouraged to empathise with his goals and re-evaluate the legitimacy of Prospero's claim to the island.

Ferdinand

In stark contrast to Miranda, **Ferdinand symbolises the role of the court and social hierarchies.** Miranda has grown up beyond this royal world (even though she is technically born into it) whereas Ferdinand has been raised as the heir of Naples. This manifests especially in his relations with Miranda. For example, his language, which is stuffy and formal (I mean, he says things like, "Noble mistress, 'tis fresh morning with me / When you are by at night") contrasts greatly with Miranda's romantic dialogue. She's incredibly straightforward and skips social norms, as seen in her no-nonsense **monosyllabic** question, "do you love me?"

Monosyllabic: words that only have one syllable.

Honestly, Ferdinand doesn't *do* very much in the play except for fall deeply and quickly in love with Miranda. He follows all the rules, obeys Prospero, and makes Miranda her queen, **therefore bringing the rule of the court to the island and allowing an exploration of Shakespeare's contextual social hierarchies.**

Alonso

Alonso's an important character to the play's exploration of revenge and imprisonment because **he suffers a very clear degradation of sanity as a result of guilt and grief.** Because of Prospero's revenge plot (which involves tricking Alonso into thinking his son is dead and a terrifying monologue by Ariel dressed as a harpy), **Alonso becomes imprisoned by his sheer remorse for his plot against Prospero.** He can only be truly free from his sins when he repents to Prospero and restores his dukedom. Only once this is done, Alonso is reintroduced to his son and all is well. He goes from being absolutely destroyed by the harpy's speech, clear in his lament "O, it is monstrous, monstrous!" to liberated by the joy he finds in a reconciliation with Prospero's family.

Gonzalo

In my opinion, Gonzalo is not only absolutely hilarious, he is also **a mirror which enables the audience to reflect on the morality and motivations of the other characters in the play.** He's the only honest character in the entire text and **his kindness only amplifies the other characters' lack of honesty.** I mean, after Gonzalo spends his first few minutes on stage trying to cheer up poor old Alonso, Antonio and Sebastian literally plot to kill him while he's sleeping.

But even though Gonzalo is technically the 'good guy', **even he isn't immune to the desire for power.** While trying to distract Alonso, Gonzalo launches into a lofty monologue about what his rule over the island would look like. He muses about his utopian ideals in language which seems to hark back to Montaigne's famous essay, *Of Cannibals*. Through the **postcolonial lens** we were talking about before, Gonzalo's speech reveals that even the 'good guys' have urges to subject others to their control and gain power by taking land.

Antonio and Sebastian

Buckle up because things are about to get super intense – it's time to discuss the Bad Guys!

Shakespeare uses Antonio and Sebastian to highlight the evil and power-hungry desires humans often grapple with. **The two are deliberately characterised indistinctly** – both are younger brothers, both are traitorous, both heckle poor Gonzalo, both are unrepentant... you get the idea. This is potentially done to **construct the two as a faceless, generic representation of the evil present in humanity.**

Their characterisation is used to critique individuals who pursue power and control over all else. Their actions are so repulsive and heinous (I mean, usurping your older brothers, plotting to kill them, and then showing no remorse) that **the audience is inherently persuaded to think of them, and therefore their nature, negatively.**

Funnily enough, Prospero too desires power and control over all else, to an extreme detriment of the people he loves. Therefore, **Antonio and Sebastian function as a mirror, enabling us to see and criticise the dark side that lives in all of the characters, and by extension, all of us.**

Stephano and Trinculo

Yes, Stephano and Trinculo are the 'funny' characters, but they actually have pretty sinister implications.

They **represent the lowest rung of society,** being a butler and jester respectively. That being said, **they act as foils to the highest rungs of society: the courtiers.** For example, their usurpation plot resembles a comedic, hopeless version of Antonio and Sebastian's usurpation plot. Both pairs want to kill Prospero and take out the top job, but Stephano and Trinculo's plan is definitely a lot less sophisticated. After all, they're literally drunk the *entire time*.

But **Stephano can also be read as a foil for Prospero himself.** Both arrive at the island and both immediately engage Caliban as a tool in their consolidation of power. While they clearly do it in different ways (Prospero with language and magic, and Stephano with alcohol) **both characters encourage the audience to think about who is the rightful owner of the island.**

Mariners, spirits, and other courtiers

The common thread through these miscellaneous background characters is that **they all further the magic and mystery of the island.** The mariners and boatswain miraculously appear untouched by the storm at the end of the play, the spirits constitute the supernatural element of the play, and the other courtiers continuously reflect on the wild and disorienting nature of the island. In doing so, **these three groups further Shakespeare's use of setting to explore themes such as revenge and imprisonment.** Ultimately, they help to construct the island as a dangerous and disturbing place which forces the guilt, motivations, and emotions of the characters to surface.

Section 5
Key Themes Analysis

Power

Power is arguably the most pervasive theme in the entire play – it dominates all discussions we have about the relationships between the characters in *The Tempest*. It seems to be the thing which **motivates every single person**, from Prospero to even good old Gonzalo. Power over people, power over land, power over magic, and power over words are all fundamental forces that govern the actions and **trajectories** of the characters.

Trajectory: the path or journey that a character undergoes over the course of the text.

Shakespeare **critiques the pursuit of unbridled power by portraying such a desire negatively**. He does this by associating the desire for power with revenge, usurpation, manipulation, and torture. To further this criticism, **Shakespeare uses the characters' emotional interior to reveal the cost that pursuing power can have on an individual.** Alonso, in particular, is an excellent example, as his demise upon being subjected to the disorienting forces of the island reveal his emotional turmoil over his past actions. On the flip side, **Shakespeare uses Antonio and Sebastian's lack of an emotional interior to condemn their actions as unempathetic, empty, and malevolent.**

Reality vs. illusions

The Tempest relies on the blurring of lines between reality and illusion to further its exploration of the human condition. This is perhaps no clearer than in the different versions of reality which exist for the courtiers – Gonzalo believes the island to be a beautiful safe haven, Alonso sees it as bleak and terrifying, and Antonio and Sebastian view it as an awful and inconvenient place. **Shakespeare furthers the ambiguity over the distinction between reality and illusion by not providing us any answers as to why different versions of the island exist.** It's up to the audience to decide whether the difference in perspective is a result of the courtiers' different personalities or whether Prospero has used magic to deliberately create different islands for each of the courtiers in order to further his revenge plan.

The ambiguity over reality versus illusion also **leads us to reconsider whether or not the histories that Prospero creates to legitimate his control are 'real'**. Perhaps, like the differences in versions of the island, there exist differences in versions of the past. After all, Prospero himself made clear that he abandoned his rule for his books, so maybe there is a different reality in which Antonio was right to usurp Prospero.

Ultimately, *The Tempest* articulates that the line between reality and illusion is pretty blurry. Shakespeare puts this down to more than just the role that magic plays, but rather the role that perspective plays.

Imprisonment

Shakespeare uses imprisonment in *The Tempest* to extrapolate some key truths about human nature. Imprisonment is inherently the opposite of freedom, which is considered the natural state of being, so by using imprisonment as all of the characters' status quo, their lives are pushed to the extreme, therefore **leading us to the extremes of humanity.**

The play explores a **multidimensional** conception of imprisonment, beginning with the **literal.** Physically, Prospero has been imprisoned on the island, forced to live out his days in the middle of the ocean. But imprisonment extends so far beyond this very literal and physical interpretation. Prospero, despite being imprisoned himself, **imprisons Caliban and Ariel through magic and his control of language.** He manipulates them through their histories, proving that imprisonment isn't an inherently physical endeavour. This is furthered by the emotional imprisonment of characters such as Alonso, who is **held from freedom by his own guilt.**

Multidimensional: something with many layers or parts.

Discovery

The Tempest isn't all doom and gloom though – the play's focus on **discovery bestows the play with an element of wonder and awe.**

We begin with the **physical discovery** of the island itself. The discovery of a setting so foreign to the courtiers' traditional environment **engenders an opportunity for transformation and self-realisation.** The context is now so far removed from what the courtiers are used to, that their environment disorients them and forces them into confrontation of their past (as clear in Alonso's case).

But, there's so much more discovery in the play than simply the physical discovery of the island. We also see Miranda break free of her innocence and absence of human interaction beyond her father to meet new people and experience new things. She manages to step out of the shadows and into a 'brave new world.' In *The Tempest,* **discovery acts as a catalyst for further discovery and resolution.** By the end of the play, most of the characters (bar Antonio and Sebastian) have undergone important self-growth, with Prospero even ready to relinquish his magic.

Language

Throughout all of Shakespeare's work, the importance of language is a pretty predominant theme, but it is perhaps dealt with most explicitly in *The Tempest*. Being a playwright, Shakespeare was well aware of how crucial control of language is, given **it was literally his job to use words to manipulate audiences into feeling how he wanted them to feel...** which sounds a lot like Prospero's use of language...

Prospero's use of language sets him up as a mirror image of Shakespeare himself. His strict control of language to control others (such as Caliban, Miranda, and Ariel) prove him to wield words just like Shakespeare does. Both are aware of the effects that language has on others and use it to their advantage, twisting words to bend the emotions of others. Prospero becomes acutely conscious of the impact his actions have had on his victims when Ariel reveals that his harpy speech has made even good old Gonzalo cry. **This awareness leads to Prospero's eventual renunciation of his staff, and thus Shakespeare's consequent renunciation of his pen.**

Revenge and forgiveness

And finally, we come to revenge and forgiveness, two sides of the same coin. When the play begins, Prospero is clearly a salty old man bent on getting revenge on those who usurped him through any means possible. He *literally* stages a storm to draw them to the island so that he can mess with their sanity!

The audience is positioned to view this exacting of revenge critically, with Prospero's taunting of the courtiers slowly hurting Alonso and Gonzalo plus Ariel and Caliban along the way. We're especially forced into questioning whether the exacting of revenge can even be considered justice at all, with Ariel representing Prospero's mouthpiece rather than a symbol of fairness and resolution. This is clear in the harpy scene, in which Ariel seems to be reciting the things that Prospero has personal gripes over rather than providing a clear moral judgement of the usurpers.

Eventually, after seeing the emotional pain he's caused (with even Ariel the spirit acknowledging he'd feel empathy for the courtiers if he were human) and realising he'll be losing his daughter to marriage, Prospero concludes that, "the rarer action is / In virtue than in vengeance." **This alliterative comparison** of "virtue" and "vengeance" **highlights forgiveness as a more favourable option than revenge**, as avenging the past only leads to actions in the present which then become deserving of revenge themselves.

Section 6

Structural Features Analysis

Setting

The island is pretty fundamental to the discovery, transformation, wonder, and tension of the play, **proving the inseparability of the text's argument from its setting.**

The island's exoticness provides an interruption to the status quo of the courtiers' lives, **forcing them into discomfort and therefore a reconsideration of their values and guilt.** Alonso in particular can no longer live with his sin because the island and his loss of Ferdinand force him to come to terms with his past. **In contrast to the rigidity and status of the royal courts, the island is a place of nature, transformation, and healing,** meaning it's a perfect setting for a play centred on the struggle between revenge and forgiveness.

The island is a deliberately ambiguous place, something which furthers the use of setting as a reflection of the play's themes. It isn't clear to the audience where exactly the island is, resulting in two effects: firstly, it adds to the portrayal of the island as a wild and mysterious place, and secondly, it bestows the play with a certain universality. Without tying it to a specific place, **Shakespeare allows for the island to serve as a metaphorical reflection of the extremes of humanity**, rather than making a contextual reference.

Binaries

Binary: something that consists of two distinctly different parts or aspects.

Shakespeare uses *tonnes* of *binaries* to amplify his exploration of power and control in *The Tempest;* in fact, it's a little alarming exactly how many binaries he uses. **He ultimately uses this binarism to develop important themes and questions by drawing parallels and differences to the audience's attention.**

We first see **a parallel between Caliban and Ariel,** Prospero's two servants. While both are imprisoned by his words and magic, and both were on the island long before Prospero, Caliban is clearly treated in a worse manner. This dualism, with Caliban representing one dimension of Prospero's interior and Ariel the other, allows for all of Prospero's mind to unfold on the stage. We see Prospero pulled between the two, either towards Caliban's darkness or Ariel's lightness, and the emotional turbulence which results.

We can also see the **binarism between the two sets of usurpers**, with Antonio and Sebastian representing high status and Stephano, Trinculo, and Caliban representing the lower. While both took aim at Prospero's life in order to pursue power, the different paths in which they chose to do so **represents the full spectrum of human nature**. From the comical to the evil, no one is excepted from the natural human desire for power, it's just about how we manage it.

These are probably the two most important binaries in the play, but there are so many that you can study: **Prospero/Stephano** (both stake unjust claim to the island), **Ferdinand/Caliban** (both are suitors of Miranda and are subjected to similar patterns of freedom/confinement), and **Prospero/Shakespeare** (as we've discussed, Prospero can potentially be read as a representation of the artist himself).

Classical unities

This is pretty much just a fancy way of saying that the principal action of the play (**unity of action**) takes place in real time (**unity of time**) in one location (**unity of place**). These three unities were coined by Aristotle in reference to a classical Greek tragedy, so **it's definitely interesting that an apparent Shakespearean comedy fits in with the conventions of a stereotypical tragedy.**

Firstly, the singular action of the play (unity of action) seems to be Prospero's exacting of revenge. Literally every single plot point is orchestrated by Prospero himself, from the tempest to his eventual reconciliation with the courtiers, revealing the revenge plot as the singular action of the play. Furthermore, this action literally corresponds with the play's run time (three hours), something which even Alonso acknowledges when he exclaims, "your eld'st acquaintance cannot be three hours," upon finding his son with Miranda. This condensing of the time frame **really boosts the tension and invites the audience into the play,** seeing as everything is happening in real time and thus right in front of them. And finally, the unity of place in *The Tempest* is pretty clear, given that the entire play takes place only on the island.

Ultimately, the classical unities of action, time, and place distinguish *The Tempest* from Shakespeare's other comedies and romances (as *The Tempest* is often called), proving the importance of this structural feature to the shaping of the text's meaning. **The classical unities create a tight, well-constructed vessel for exploration of the text's main themes.**

Motifs

Magic

The use of magic as a motif **denotes Prospero's interference with the natural order**, so each time it appears **the audience is forced to acknowledge Prospero's continuous manipulation and control of others.** That being said, magic also drives the plot forward, signalling a departure from the old and into the new. In this way, **the motif of magic constructs Prospero as the playwright, and not just the magician.** It is he who, through magic, calls the shots, casts illusions, and restores peace, just like the playwright does with his pen. In this way, **the motif stands in for Shakespeare's career and art, especially when we read Prospero's renunciation of magic as Shakespeare's renunciation of writing.**

But magic can also be read as a **motif for control.** Prospero routinely uses his magic to abuse the power balance in his relationships: he sends Miranda to sleep whenever he wishes, orchestrates the meeting between Miranda and Ferdinand, forces Caliban to obey him through curses, and emotionally tortures his enemies through Ariel. So, while Prospero's use of magic is characterised as 'good' in comparison to Sycorax's 'dark' magic, **the motif makes clear the ambiguity which cloaks Prospero's role in the play.**

Music

And the final important structural feature in *The Tempest* is its use of music. Music is often overlooked in Shakespeare's plays, especially as students tend to read the play rather than see it in action. **But music is absolutely integral to this play, given that it demarcates and furthers the text's exploration of key themes.**

Music underscores some of the most beautiful and poignant moments of the play – the main one that comes to mind is Caliban's brilliant speech about the island, Not only does Ariel play music while the scene progresses, **Caliban in fact bestows the island with a musical and lyrical quality in surprisingly poetic language:** "the isle is full of noises, / Sounds, and sweet airs, that give delight and hurt now. / Sometimes a thousand twangling instruments / Will hum about mine ears."

But the music of the play doesn't just play a background role which helps to jazz the text up, **it also plays a pretty integral role in the development of the plot.** It draws Ferdinand to Miranda, sends Alonso and Gonzalo to sleep so Antonio and Sebastian could plot to kill them, and further degrades the sanity of the courtiers. (Plus, the songs themselves have some pretty nice lyrics!)

Section 7

Quote Bank

Power and control

Quote	Character	Act/Scene
"Thou liest, malignant thing! Hast thou forgot / The foul witch Sycorax"	Prospero	Act 1 Scene 2
"If thou more murmur'st, I will rend an oak / And peg thee in his knotty entrails till / Thou hast howled away twelve winters."	Prospero	Act 1 Scene 2
"For this, be sure, tonight thou shalt have cramps, / Side-stiches, that shall pen thy breath up; urchins / Shall, for that vast of night that they may work, / All exercise on thee"	Prospero	Act 1 Scene 2
"This island's mine, by Sycorax my mother, / Which thou tak'st from me."	Caliban	Act 1 Scene 2
"When thou cam'st first / Thou strok'st me, and made much of me; wouldst give me / Water with berries in't, and teach me how / To name the bigger light, and how the less, / That burn by day and night. And then I loved thee, / And showed thee all the qualities o'th'isle, / The fresh springs, brine-pits, barren place and fertile – / Cursed be that I did so!"	Caliban	Act 1 Scene 2
"I must obey. His art is of such power, / It would control my dam's god Setebos, / And make a vassal of him."	Caliban	Act 2 Scene 2
"That's a brave god, and bears celestial liquor. I will kneel to him."	Caliban	Act 2 Scene 2
"I'll show thee the best springs. I'll pluck thee berries. / I'll fish for thee, and get thee wood enough. / A plague upon the tyrant that I serve!"	Caliban	Act 2 Scene 2
"I am subject to a tyrant, a sorcerer that by his cunning hath cheated me of the island."	Caliban	Act 3 Scene 2

Family

Quote	Character	Act/Scene
"I have done nothing but in care of thee – / Of thee, my dear one, thee my daughter"	Prospero	Act 1 Scene 2
"Here in this island we arrived, and here / Have I, thy schoolmaster, made thee more profit / Than other princes can, that have more time / For vainer hours, and tutors not so careful."	Prospero	Act 1 Scene 2
"I know thou canst not choose"	Prospero	Act 1 Scene 2

Ambition

Quote	Character	Act/Scene
"My strong imagination sees a crown / Dropping upon thy head."	Antonio	Act 2 Scene 1
"A space whose every cubit / Seems to cry out, 'How shall that Claribel / Measure us back to Naples? Keep in Tunis, / And let Sebastian wake'."	Antonio	Act 2 Scene 1
"As thou got'st Milan, I'll come by Naples."	Sebastian	Act 2 Scene 1

Discovery

Quote	Character	Act/Scene
"Lord, how it looks about! Believe me, sir, / It carries a brave form. But 'tis a spirit."	Miranda	Act 1 Scene 2
"We are such stuff as dreams are made on, and our little life / Is rounded with a sleep."	Prospero	Act 4 Scene 1
"All torment, trouble, wonder, and amazement / Inhabits here."	Gonzalo	Act 5 Scene 1
"O wonder! / How many goodly creatures are there here! / How beauteous mankind is! O brave new world, / That has such people in't!"	Miranda	Act 5 Scene 1
"'Tis new to thee."	Prospero	Act 5 Scene 1

Quote	Character	Act/Scene
"In one voyage / Did Claribel her husband find at Tunis, / And Ferdinand her brother found a wife / Where he himself was lost; Prospero his dukedom / In a poor isle; and all of us ourselves, / When no man was his own."	Gonzalo	Act 5 Scene 1

Love and marriage

Quote	Character	Act/Scene
"Poor worm, thou art infected!"	Prospero	Act 3 Scene 1
"Do you love me?"	Miranda	Act 3 Scene 1
"I am your wife, if you will marry me; / If not, I'll die your maid. To be your fellow / You may deny me, but I'll be your servant / Whether you will or no."	Miranda	Act 3 Scene 1
"But / If thou dost break her virgin-knot before / All sanctimonious ceremonies may / With full and holy rite be ministered."	Prospero	Act 4 Scene 1

Morality

Quote	Character	Act/Scene
"I thus neglecting worldly ends, all dedicated / To closeness and the bettering of my mind / With that which, but by being so retired, / O'er-prized all popular rate, in my false brother / Awaked an evil nature."	Prospero	Act 1 Scene 2
"So of his gentleness, / Knowing I loved my books, he furnished me / From mine own library with volumes that / I prize above my dukedom."	Prospero	Act 1 Scene 2
"Who, though they are of monstrous shape, yet note / Their manners are more gentle, kind, than of / Our human generation you shall find / Many, nay almost any."	Gonzalo	Act 3 Scene 3

Quote	Character	Act/Scene
"You are three men of sin, whom destiny, / That hath to instrument this lower world / And what is in't, the never-surfeited sea / Hath caused to belch up you."	Ariel	Act 3 Scene 3
"Methought the billows spoke, and told me of it, / The winds did sing it to me, and the thunder, / That deep and dreadful organ-pipe, pronounced / The name of Prosper."	Alonso	Act 3 Scene 3
"All three of them are desperate. Their great guilt, / Like poison given to work a great time after, Now 'gins to bite the spirits."	Gonzalo	Act 3 Scene 3

Revenge and forgiveness

Quote	Character	Act/Scene
"Sometime I'd divide / And burn in many places; on the topmast, / The yards and bowsprit, would I flame distinctly, / Then meet and join."	Ariel	Act 1 Scene 2
"All the infections that the sun sucks up / From bogs, fens, flats, on Prosper fall, and make him / By inch-meal a disease!"	Caliban	Act 2 Scene 2
"There thou mayst brain him, / Having first seized his books; or with a log / Batter his skull, or paunch him with a stake, / Or cut his weasand with thy knife."	Caliban	Act 3 Scene 2
"I have made you mad."	Ariel	Act 3 Scene 3
"But remember – / For that's my business to you – that you three / From Milan did supplant good Prospero."	Ariel	Act 3 Scene 3
"The good old lord Gonzalo. / His tears run down his beard like winter's drops / From eaves of reeds."	Ariel	Act 5 Scene 1
"Your charm so strongly works 'em / That, if you now beheld them, your affections / Would become tender."	Ariel	Act 5 Scene 1
"The rarer action is / In virtue than in vengeance."	Prospero	Act 5 Scene 1

Quote	Character	Act/Scene
"For you, most wicked sir, whom to call brother / Would even infect my mouth, I do forgive / Thy rankest fault – all of them – and require / My dukedom of thee, which perforce I know / Thou must restore."	Prospero	Act 5 Scene 1

Language

Quote	Character	Act/Scene
"I pitied thee, / Took pains to make thee speak, taught thee each hour / One thing or other."	Miranda	Act 1 Scene 2
"You taught me language, and my profit on't / Is, I know how to curse. The red plague ride you / For learning me your language!"	Caliban	Act 1 Scene 2
"My language? Heavens! / I am the best of them that speak this speech, / Were I but where 'tis spoken."	Ferdinand	Act 1 Scene 2
"Now my charms are all o'erthrown, / And what strength I have's mine own, / Which is most faint."	Prospero	Epilogue

Magic and illusions

Quote	Character	Act/Scene
"The ditty does remember my drowned father. / This is no mortal business, nor no sound / That the earth owes."	Ferdinand	Act 1 Scene 2
"How lush and lusty the grass looks! How green!"	Gonzalo	Act 2 Scene 1
"Me thinks our garments are now as fresh as when we put them on first in Afric, at the marriage of the King's fair daughter Claribel to the King of Tunis."	Gonzalo	Act 2 Scene 1
"Be not afeard; the isle is full of noises, / Sounds, and sweet airs, that give delight and hurt not. / Sometimes a thousand twangling instruments / Will hum about mine ears."	Caliban	Act 3 Scene 3

Quote	Character	Act/Scene
"Now I will believe / That there are unicorns."	Sebastian	Act 3 Scene 3
"Graces at my command / Have waked their sleepers, oped and let 'em forth / By my so potent art."	Prospero	Act 5 Scene 1
"But this rough magic / I here abjure; and when I have required some heavenly music – which even now I do – / To work mine end upon their senses that / This ariy charm is for, I'll break my staff, / Bury it certain fathoms in the earth, / And deeper than did ever plummet sound / I'll drown my book."	Prospero	Act 5 Scene 1
"I do forgive thee, / Unnatural though thou art."	Prospero	Act 5 Scene 1

Loss

Quote	Character	Act/Scene
"Sitting on a bank, / Weeping again the King my father's wreck, / This music crept by me upon the waters, / Allaying both their fury and my passion / With its sweet air."	Ferdinand	Act 1 Scene 2
"Would I had never / Married my daughter there! For, coming thence, / My son is lost, and, in my rate, she too, / Who is so far from Italy removed / I ne'er again shall see her."	Alonso	Act 2 Scene 1
"Even here I will put off my hope, and keep it / No longer for my flatterer. He is drowned / Whom thus we stray to find, and the sea mocks / Our frustrate search on land."	Alonso	Act 3 Scene 3
"As great to me, as late; and supportable / To make the dear loss... For I have lost my daughter."	Prospero	Act 5 Scene 1

Section 8

Sample Essays

Essay One

QUESTION: To what extent does *The Tempest's* significance arise from its exploration of the tension between revenge and forgiveness?

ESSAY	COMMENTS
INTRODUCTION Revenge and forgiveness form an important binary at the heart of questions about human nature and morality – the tension between the two therefore proving a source for timeless and universal exploration.[1] Thus, William Shakespeare's 17th century romance, *The Tempest* – a play driven by protagonist Prospero's turmoil over avenging past wrongs[2] – draws its significance to a high extent from its sophisticated interrogation of the interplay between revenge and forgiveness.[4] In the play, Shakespeare effectively employs the dramatic form to invite the audience into a consideration of the morality of revenge and a revaluation of whether Caliban's actions are worthy of forgiveness, proving the centrality of the binary to the play's meaning. Furthermore, Prospero's pursuit of revenge and forgiveness essentially drives the plot forward, enriching the text by allowing questions over Prospero's potential representation of the role of the playwright.[5] Ultimately, the tension between revenge and forgiveness imbues the play with timeless question, therefore constituting to a high extent the play's significance.	1. This opening sentence provides a useful foundation by unpacking the prompt's key terms and linking them with the idea of what comprises textual integrity (e.g. timelessness and universality, to name a few). 2. Without getting into too much detail, we here characterise some manifestations of revenge and forgiveness to show the marker we understand what these words mean in relation to the play itself. 3. We have also used words like 'interplay' in order to unpack the idea of 'tension' that the prompt mentions. Don't underestimate any part of the essay question, as often these seemingly insignificant words can in fact lead to very sophisticated discussions! 4. Note that we are maintaining a focus on the themes of revenge and forgiveness – writing an introduction that is highly relevant to the prompt should be your first priority when you compose your piece in the exam, since this is what the markers will be looking for! 5. This expansion of ideas will help us transition into our first body paragraph.

PARAGRAPH 1

Shakespeare successfully employs a variety of dramatic features to cast ambiguity over the morality of revenge, a depiction which strengthens the play's textual integrity, and thus its significance.[6] The play portrays the sheer impact of revenge on Prospero's enemies by inviting the audience to experience the same horror and bewilderment the lost courtiers experience on the island,[7] described by Gonzalo as a 'fearful country.' The impact of Prospero's vengeful magic on Alonso is clear in his fearful anthropomorphic[8] description of the island after the harpy speech: "The winds did sing it to me, and the thunder, / That deep and dreadful organ-pipe, pronounced / The name of Prosper." The horrors of the island have so degraded his sanity by this point in the play that he admits he wants to commit suicide so he can join his son Ferdinand, who he believes dead, lamenting "I'll seek him deeper than e'er plummet sounded, / And with him there lie mudded." This rhyming couplet[9] bestows his decision with a sense of finality, proving the overwhelmingly emotional impact Prospero's search for revenge has had on him. The audience is encouraged to feel empathetic for Alonso, and thus condemn Prospero's revenge,[10] due to the play's adoption of the classical unities, particularly the unity of time. The unfolding of action in real time enables the audience to experience the torment of the island as the courtiers experience it, rather than it being relayed back to them through dialogue, thus begging a more personal reaction.

6. This topic sentence not only clearly outlines the focus for this paragraph's argument, but also explicitly ties this to the prompt and the core question about *The Tempest's* significance.

7. Rather than only analysing characters and dialogue (as is the case in most mid-range essays), we're stepping back to incorporate the audience's response, and more specifically, how Shakespeare wants audiences to respond to certain elements of his play, and hence why he has constructed characters and presented their dialogue in particular ways. This scope is something typically only seen in high-range pieces, so considering the authorial intent and audience reception is a great way to enhance your essays!

8. This is a highly specific technique that showcases our understanding of the play's language features.

9. It's always good to be as precise as possible with your quoting – here, we're specifically talking about the effect of Alonso's rhyming couplet, so both lines have been quoted in full.

10. Here we have directly acknowledged the intended effect of Shakespeare's authorial decisions, and have explained the meaning of this evidence in terms of what the audience think and feel.

Ultimately, this evocation of empathy through Alonso's degradation of sanity and use of classical unities are employed by Shakespeare to cast doubt[11] over the morality of revenge, thus providing a rich discourse from which the text draws its significance to a high extent.

PARAGRAPH 2
Having cast doubt on Prospero's morality,[12] Shakespeare then invites the audience to reconsider whether Caliban's search for revenge is then justified and his usurpation actions worthy of forgiveness, adding even greater layers of depth to the play. From Caliban's first scene, Shakespeare foregrounds[13] questions about whether Prospero's control over the island, and consequent oppression of Caliban, is legitimate or justified. The cruelty of Prospero's control over Caliban, as revealed through his excessive listing[14] of curses as seen in 'tonight thou shalt have cramps, / Side-stiches, that shall pen thy breath up; urchins" is contrasted with Caliban's genuine claim to ownership of the island. Caliban's close relationship with the island is particularly intimated through his use of auditorily rich verse, as he confides "the isle is full of noises, / Sounds, and sweet airs, that give delight and hurt not." He further characterises the island's soundscape as "a thousand twangling instruments... hum[ming] about [his][15] ears." This verse poignantly emphasises the legitimacy of Caliban's claim to the island in comparison to Prospero's, thus suggesting to the audience that Caliban's revenge plot against his master, who has exploited him to great detriment, is perhaps forgivable.

11. This is a very effective concluding sentence that links the overarching example (Alonso's trajectory throughout the play) to the intention and impact, using Shakespeare's name and verbs like 'employed' and 'providing' to signal this summary of our analysis.
12. Right away, this paragraph opens with a seamless incorporation of the previous discussion, tying it into our next point. Though it's vital for your topic sentences to outline what the paragraph is about, being able to bridge the gaps between your paragraphs by including a linking phrase likes this is a cherry on top!
13. This is a great very to describe how Shakespeare makes things obvious (it literally means 'bring to the foreground' or highlight to the audience!).
14. Although it may not seem like a conventional technique like 'metaphors' or 'alliteration,' grammatical and rhetorical features like 'listing' are also completely valid forms of metalanguage that you can employ throughout your analysis.
15. Note the modification of the quote here to suit this sentence.

This tension between revenge and forgiveness therefore enables a nuanced interpretation of Caliban's character, further proving the text's significance a result of this binary's dynamic to a high extent.

PARAGRAPH 3

Prospero's search for revenge, and eventual choice to pursue forgiveness and thus renounce magic, forms part of his character's construction as a dramatisation of Shakespeare himself, thereby imbuing the play with a metatheatricality[16] and highly enriching its significance. *The Tempest* is structured around the classical unities of action, time, and place, with the singular action being Prospero's revenge plot. Hence, just as a dramatist does, Prospero guides the plot of the play with this singular action, beginning with his orchestration of the tempest itself.[17] As Ariel reports his enaction of Prospero's vengeful commands with the metaphorical recounting of "yards and bowspirit" that he would "flame distinctly, / Then meet and join," Prospero's ability to create a dramatic spectacle becomes clear. Prospero's consistent manipulation of the natural order, from sending Miranda to sleep because he "know[s she] canst not choose," to his confrontation of his enemies,[18] reveals his complete control over the plot, thereby enabling a reading of Prospero as a representation of Shakespeare himself. Prospero finally acknowledges that forgiveness is a more moral choice than revenge, admitting "the rarer action is / In virtue than in vengeance," and in doing so draws his plot, and therefore *The Tempest's* plot, to a close.[19]

16. This fancy word just refers to the aspects of the play that draw attention or show an awareness of the fact that it is a play. (Prospero's final speech is a good example of this!)

17. This is where we explain our thinking in order to justify this interpretation of Prospero's role. Remember that you can't take for granted that your assessor will join the dots for you – it's your responsibility to ensure your ideas are well-substantiated and clearly conveyed.

18. Here, we've chained together multiple examples in order to strengthen this idea and analysis.

19. Be careful when interpreting Prospero in this way, as you don't want to get too caught up in the metatheatricality and end up confusing your assessor! But so long as you can clearly express your thoughts and talk about the character's role confidently, you should be fine!

This triumph of forgiveness over revenge, and the consequent renunciation of magic, if Prospero's character is read as a metaphor for Shakespeare, mirrors the dramatist's decision to end his career and renounce the pen. In this way, the tension between revenge and forgiveness opens a reading of the play as Shakespeare's swansong to his career, and proves once more the tension as play's main source of significance to a high extent.

CONCLUSION

Ultimately, Shakespeare's sophisticated exploration of the dynamic between revenge and forgiveness invites the audience into a nuanced interpretation of *The Tempest,* thereby proving the play's significance to a high extent a result of the binary's tension. By opening the possibility for empathy with the courtiers over Prospero's cruel exactment of revenge, the audience is encouraged to doubt the morality of the protagonist and in doing so, imbues the text with a richer meaning.[20] Furthermore, Prospero's ambiguous morality then allows a reinterpretation of Caliban's character, inviting the audience to perceive his revenge plot as forgivable. But it is perhaps Prospero's driving of the plot through his inner turmoil over revenge and forgiveness which provides the play with the most significance, as it allows a parallel to be drawn between the magician and the dramatist himself. Thus, through its evocation of complex moral questions and metatheatricality, *The Tempest* is proven to draw its textual integrity to a high extent from its interrogation of the tension between revenge and forgiveness.

20. As with any good conclusion, this paragraph briefly revisits the core components of this essay's arguments, threading them all together into an impressive thesis. Remember to never introduce any new evidence or interpretations in your conclusion – you should instead be building off of the analysis you've provided up until this point, and rounding out your discussion with 'big picture' ideas about what meaning the text imparts to audiences, and/or how the play's textual integrity is ultimately used to convey certain ideas.

Essay Two

QUESTION: 'Confronting and provocative discoveries often have transformative effects.' To what extent does The Tempest support this statement?

ESSAY	COMMENTS
INTRODUCTION Discoveries,[1] especially ones that force the discover into a state of discomfort and vulnerability, have the potential to uproot long-held assumptions and beliefs, leading to self-growth and realisation. This notion is perhaps no clearer than in William Shakespeare's 17th century work *The Tempest,* a text deeply grounded in the transformative effects of confronting and provocative discoveries. Through the discomforting, and at times traumatic,[2] physical discovery of the island the courtiers undergo serious transformation, having been removed from their traditional contexts. The transformative potential of confronting discoveries is further explored through Miranda's realisation of a world beyond the one presented by her father. But the audience too is invited into The Tempest's exploration of the inextricable connection between provocative discoveries and transformation, with a reconsideration of Caliban's character through the powerful realisation of empathy for his plight. Ultimately, the text's deft exploration of this connection supports the statement to a high extent.[3]	1. Again, the introduction engages with key words in the prompt from the outset. Although this opening sentence is just providing an ideological starting point before we delve into the text, it is still conveying to the marker that we have closely read the essay question and are responding to it directly. 2. Notice how we are using both the prompt's key words (confronting and provocative) as well as synonyms (discomforting and traumatic)? This helps us demonstrate our *comprehension* of the prompt (i.e. we're not just regurgitating the language used in the question – we truly understand what it means, and are furthering our discussion through the use of more specific related terms!). 3. Don't be afraid to tackle the prompt's core question head-on! It's always better to err on the side of caution so that your thesis comes across clearly and without ambiguity.

PARAGRAPH 1

The physical discovery of a discomforting and exotic location, such as the island, has the potential to lead to significant transformation due to its forcing of a break from the status quo, proving the statement integral to *The Tempest*. The provocative and confronting[4] nature of the island is revealed through the courtiers' reactions, beginning with their differing perspectives of the location. Gonzalo, for example, exclaims, "how lush and lusty the grass looks! How green!" which contrasts greatly[5] with Antonio's view, who instead dryly remarks, "the ground, indeed, is tawny." The lack of certainty with which the audience is provided pertaining to what the island actually looks like engenders an environment of unease and disorientation,[6] an environment which separates the courtiers from the status quo and forces them to reconsider their values. Alonso's transformation on the island exemplifies this connection between a confronting physical discovery and growth, with his sanity's demise at the hands of the island leading to his reconciliation with Prospero. After being worn down by his search for his lost son on the treacherous island and the harpy's terrifying monology, Alonso's sheer reaction to the provocative discovery of the island is revealed in his repetitious lament,[7] "O, it is monstrous, monstrous!" This reaction reveals[8] his complete degradation at the hands of the island's provocative forces and his acceptance of guilt.

4. Remember to incorporate the essay question's key words and ideas consistently throughout your essay (don't just chuck them in the introduction and then forget about them!) A *sustained* focus on the prompt is guaranteed to impress your marker!

5. Use linking words to highlight the similarity or differences between different quotes and examples – this makes your analysis seem far more fluent than other essays that merely analyse each technique in isolation before moving on to the next.

6. In addition to talking about things that are confronting and provocative for the characters, you can add another dimension to your analysis and discuss how things are confronting and provocative to the audience too!

7. More good metalanguage here to introduce this quote.

8. And the quote is instantly followed up with a sentence explaining its significance! This is a great habit to get into for English, as it ensures you'll never lose marks for failing to analyse any evidence you include in your essays!

This positions him well for a positive transformation of character in the final scene, in which he immediately returns Prospero's dukedom and repents upon finding him alive: "Thy dukedom I resign, and do entreat / Thou pardon me my wrongs." Thus,[9] Alonso's transformation upon being subjected to the disquieting and unnerving discovery of the island are testaments to the importance of the statement to the play.

PARAGRAPH 2
The confronting realisation of a world beyond one's familiarity also[10] has the propensity for an upheaval of an individual's identity and role; an integral concept to the development of Miranda's character in The Tempest. In Act 1 Scene 2, Miranda is introduced to the audience through the prism of innocence[11] – it is clear she has come of age within the confines of the world created by her father, Prospero. This is demonstrated in Miranda's revelation that Prospero had "often / Begun to tell me what I am, but stopped, / And left me to a bootless inquisition, / Concluding, 'Stay; not yet." This witty insight reveals Prospero's tight control over Miranda's awareness of the world – something furthered[12] by his remark , 'I know thou canst not choose,' when he sends her to sleep. This tight control of Miranda's perspective makes her discovery of Ferdinand, the first man she's ever seen besides her father and Caliban, all the more confronting, and thus, all the more transformative. So overwhelmed by the discovery's provocative nature, she falls instantly in love, beginning her transformation from a naïve young girl under her father's control to a woman, soon to be married to the heir of Naples.

9. Before ending your paragraph with an impactful concluding statement, try to use a word like 'thus' or 'therefore' to signal your intent – this just makes it easier for your marker to see that you've ended by taking things back to the essay question and your thesis!

10. Even using a simple word like 'also' in places like this can aid your essay's fluency, and connects one paragraph's discussion to the analysis you've previously conducted.

11. Though not a huge part of the marking scheme, it's good to order your evidence in a sensible way (i.e. talking about how Miranda as a character is first introduced to the audience before discussing her progression and the dynamic of her relationship with Prospero and others).

12. In addition, the word 'furthered' is another great linking word when chaining together similar examples that all contribute to the same theme or characterisation.

The provocative nature of this discovery is revealed through her forward interactions with Ferdinand, particularly her monosyllabic question, "do you love me?" Her language contrasts greatly with Ferdinand's eloquent and formal dialogue, further conveying to the audience the confronting effect this discovery of a world outside her awareness, and love, on Miranda. This discovery, Shakespeare intimates,[13] leads to her ultimate transformation from Prospero's daughter to Ferdinand's queen, confirming *The Tempest's* high support of the statement.

PARAGRAPH 3

The interpretation of characters themselves are not exempt from the transformative effects of a provocative discovery,[14] as clear through the reconsideration of Caliban made possible through the confronting realisation of a postcolonial[15] reading of *The Tempest*. While Caliban is at a superficial level portrayed as the antagonist, with his usurpation plot against Prospero and other characters' continuous reference to him as a "slave" and "monster" contributing to a negative conception, the audience's potentially shocking discovery of empathy for Caliban[16] through a postcolonial reading opens the door for a transformation of understandings. A postcolonial reading of the play engenders an understanding of Caliban as the true owner of the island, with Caliban's furious outburst, "I am subject to a tyrant, a sorcerer that by his cunning hath cheated me of the island," serving a poignant reminder of his unfair and cruel treatment at the hands of Prospero's illegitimate claim to the island.

13. In order to avoid lapsing into summary and merely retelling the plot, you should make frequent reference to Shakespeare (and/or the audience, or the play's title) as this forces you to make a more analytical comment about the play as a construct.

14. This is a slightly different take on the prompt, and definitely something you would want to leave for a third or fourth body paragraph (instead of a first or second!). But now that we have sufficiently discussed the provocative and confronting elements of the characters and plot, we are now able to talk about more complex ideas like the provocative and confronting alternate interpretations of characters!

15. Although you can safely assume that your marker will know what words like this mean, it never hurts to clarify them over the course of your analysis. If nothing else, it will affirm to your reader that you understand the term and can apply it to the play.

16. This is a highly sophisticated analysis of audience reception and how we are made to feel about the characters over the course of the play!

This is furthered by the parallels drawn between Prospero and the drunken Stephano, a binary[17] which highlights the exploitation of indigenous peoples in Shakespeare's time, as alarmingly clear in Caliban's invocation of divinity regarding drunken Stephano, 'That's a brave god, and bears celestial liquor. I will kneel to him.' In this way,[18] a postcolonial reading leads to the troubling discovery of Prospero's potentially antagonistic underbelly and thus a transformation in the way Caliban is understood by the audience and the critic, ultimately proving the centrality of the statement to the text.

CONCLUSION

Provocative and confronting discoveries are rife with opportunity for deep transformation, a notion supported to a high extent by Shakespeare's *The Tempest*.[19] The statement is clearly integral to the play's textual sophistication, with the confronting discovery of the exotic and discomforting island leading to profound character transformation. Furthermore, Miranda's provocative encounter with Ferdinand leads her to the realisation of a world beyond her boundaries of experience, resulting in a significant growth in character spurred by the subsequent discovery of love. But the audience too is invited to make powerful and disquieting discoveries through the realisation of empathy for Caliban made possible by a postcolonial reading. Ultimately,[20] Shakespeare's harnessing of the deeply forceful ramifications of discovery constructs an exquisite exploration of the central truth provided in the statement – that provocative and confronting discoveries can uproot and transform an individual.

17. You don't always have to use a sentence structure like 'Shakespeares use of binaries can be seen in the quote...' A more flexible approach to weaving in techniques, as seen here, can greatly enhance your writing, and will make things more dynamic and varied for your assessor too!

18. Since we're approaching the end of this paragraph, and indeed the end of the essay, it's important to guide your marker to your overarching conclusion. By this point, you will have done a great deal of work in setting up your ideas, so make sure you do those ideas justice in the final moments of your essay!

19. The start of your conclusion should be directed towards the prompt so that there is absolutely no doubt that you have answered the question in its entirety.

20. The end of your conclusion should zoom out to Shakspeare's commentary about the core themes.

Essay Three

QUESTION: How does William Shakespeare explore power and corruption in *The Tempest*?

ESSAY	COMMENTS
INTRODUCTION *The Tempest,* William Shakespeare's 17th century romance play, traces its enduring relevance and value to its multidimensional and complex exploration of the workings of power and corruption.[1] Centred on the revenge plot of its protagonist, Prospero, *The Tempest* relies on its interrogation of the uses and abuses of power[2] to speak both to its contextual and modern audiences. This exploration is enabled through Shakespeare's effective employment of imprisonment to analyse the corruption of Prospero's power and its human effects. As the devastation of such a corruption is established, Shakespeare simultaneously uses binaries to amplify the proliferation of the abuses of control in society. Furthermore, the text effectively explores the ability of language to manipulate and control others to reinforce the play's exploration of such poignant themes. Through this array of explorative devices, Shakespeare highlights the potential for the natural human desire to accumulate power to mutate into moral corruption.[3]	1. This introduction is another good example of opening with a direct addressing of the prompt. 2. Here, we've added some complexity to the discussion by unpacking different manifestations of power (i.e. using and abusing power). This helps us maintain relevance to the question, but also lead the discussion towards related ideas, such as magic and illusion, or Prospero's role as a manipulator). 3. Notice how this introduction goes further than merely saying 'yes, Shakespeare explores power and corruption!' When you get a seemingly straightforward prompt like this, it usually means you will need to craft your own, more complex argument in order to flesh out your thesis.

PARAGRAPH 1

Shakespeare draws upon the imprisonment of the courtiers, Ariel, and Caliban to reflect upon the effects of Prospero's corruption of power, inviting the audience into a moral indictment of such a development. Beginning in Act 1 Scene 2, Prospero's strict imprisonment of Ariel, a spirit of the island, is cast as morally ambiguous.[4] After reminding Prospero of his promise to free Ariel, Prospero erupts, posing the manipulative question "dost though forget / From what a torment I did free thee?" When Ariel responds that he hasn't, Prospero exclaims, "thou liest, malignant thing!" This abusive language[5] contrasts greatly[6] with that of Ariel's dialogue, such as, 'I thank thee, master,' which instead possesses a respectful tone. This contrast, as well as Prospero's cruel enslavement of the true owner of the island, Caliban, encourages the audience to adopt a negative perception of Prospero's use of power. Prospero's disproportionate[7] responses to Caliban's testing of boundaries, as clear in Prospero's violent threats such as, 'I'll rack thee with old cramps, / Fill all thy ones with aches, make thee roar / That beasts shall tremble at thy din,' further this perception. But it is perhaps[8] Shakespeare's exploration of the impact of Prospero's imprisonment of the courtiers which is most significant to the development of the play's moral argument. For example, Ariel's use of the visual imagery to report the likeable Gonzalo's emotional state at being imprisoned – "his tears run down his beard like winter's drops / From eaves of reeds" – draws an empathetic reaction for the sufferer of the abuse of power, rather than its perpetuator, Prospero.

4. We're also relating the themes of power and control to the question of morality, since *The Tempest* doesn't have neat distinctions between 'good power' and 'bad power.' You should use these blurred lines to your advantage, as talking about the moral greyness in the play will definitely add sophistication to your analysis!

5. Here, we are only quoting the most relevant language, rather than huge chunks of the dialogue. This precision allows us to then earn more marks for close analysis.

6. And again, the use of comparative linking language lets us seamlessly transition from one example to another.

7. This is a subtle way to communicate your interpretation. Here, this adjective expresses our reading of Prospero's character as one who abuses his power, without needing to explicitly state this.

8. Remember that you don't have to be extremely definitive when it comes to matters of interpretation. In fact, markers tend to prefer it when you use low modal language like this, as it implies you understand the text's complexity and you haven't oversimplified its messages.

Furthermore, the state of the courtiers' upon being imprisoned not only draws an empathetic response from the audience, but also from Ariel, who confesses he would feel sorry for them "were I human." This refraction of the suffering at the hands of Prospero's corruption through the prism of imprisonment develops Shakespeare's[9] compelling exploration of the human effects the accumulation of power can have.

PARAGRAPH 2
Shakespeare, however, is careful to not rely on Prospero as the sole vessel for exploration of power and corruption,[10] instead employing binaries to reflect the proliferation of these two themes throughout society. There is a deliberate[11] parallel between Antonio and Caliban, both characters who fall prey to their ambition and seek to displace Prospero from power. Antonio's actions are clearly condemned, especially by Prospero, who refers to him repeatedly as "evil." Antonio's corruption, along with Sebastian's and Alonso's,[12] is further condemned in the language of the harpy speech, with Ariel powerfully declaring "you are three men of sin." This monosyllabic accusation bluntly and forcefully associates ambition, and consequent corruption, with a religious offence,[13] something which would have resonated with the text's contextual audience. This is furthered by the binarism of Antonio's character with Caliban, with the actions of each character reflecting and enriching Shakespeare's exploration of the proliferation of corruption within society. While Antonio represents the highest rung of society, Caliban represents the lowest, yet both fall prey to the natural human desire to accumulate power.

9. Use the author's name in your concluding sentences. (This isn't a 'rule' per se, but it is a good habit that ensures your paragraph ends are addressing the author's role in creating textual integrity!)
10. Never disregard the other characters in the play. Even though Prospero seems like the most obvious choice when discussing themes like power and control, you should integrate other characters into your discussion too, as your essay needs to encompass a broad scope of examples.
11. This tells the assessor we are acknowledging Shakespeare's role as a composer, and the fact that everything in the play is the product of his purposeful authorial intent.
12. Here, we are grouping together related ideas (specifically the perceived corruption of these three characters) in order to analyse them all efficiently but effectively.
13. Note the step-by-step explanation of this quote's significance? This is time-consuming, but is *incredibly* valuable as it demonstrates every skill the markers want to see!

While both characters' actions are condemned, they are done so in different ways,[14] with Antonio's clearly criticised as a sin, and Caliban's characterised as a ridiculous farce. This is done through Caliban's association with the two comedic drunks, Stephano and Trinculo, and his ultimate feeble attempt. Even Caliban recognises his failings, invoking a mythological allusion: "O Setebos, these be brave spirits indeed! / How fine my master is! I am afraid / He will chastise me." Ultimately, Shakespeare's use of binaries furthers his nuanced exploration[15] of power and corruption in *The Tempest*.

PARAGRAPH 3

In a metatheatrical approach,[16] Shakespeare furthers this exploration through a reflection on the ability for language to both corrupt and be corrupted. This is made clear through Prospero's rigorous control of language in his maintenance of power and abuse. For example, when Prospero tells his daughter Miranda of their history, he does so in a way that legitimates his morality and condemns his perceived enemies. This is particularly clear in Prospero's positioning of himself as morally superior to his usurping brother, who he says had "an evil nature" for taking over the throne, despite Prospero in fact neglecting his rule for the "bettering of my mind."[17] Prospero's legitimation of power through his corruption of language is furthered in his dialogue with Ariel, in which he invokes a morally charged version of history, contrasting his "light" magic with the "dark" magic of the previous resident of the island, Sycorax.

14. In addition to linking together different examples, you can also create fluency and cohesion within your paragraphs by challenging ideas like this, and pointing out differences in their significance or effect.

15. As always, the paragraph conclusions should take things back to the author, your thesis, and the essay question.

16. You may notice that the especially layered or complicated ideas like metatheatricality are often left for the final body paragraph – this is by design! You don't want to attempt a discussion of these too early, or before you have set the groundwork in other paragraphs. However, by the time you get to your third body paragraph, you'll hopefully have the confidence and an adequate analytical foundation to talk about bigger ideas like these!

17. This paragraph uses fairly short quotes, which draws attention to how precise the analysis is.

Using possessive language[18] in his declaration, "It was mine art, / When I arrived and heard thee, that made gap / The pine, and let thee out," Prospero positions himself as morally superior to Sycorax's magic and in doing so, consolidates his control over Ariel through words.[19] This exploration of the corruption of language furthers Shakespeare's sophisticated interrogation of power, enriching the play's textual integrity and lasting relevance.

CONCLUSION

Ultimately, Shakespeare constructs a meaningful and sophisticated exploration of power and corruption, drawing upon his mastering of the dramatic form to present a persuasive didactic text. This exploration is firstly[20] made possible through the use of imprisonment within the text, amplifying the effects of power and corruption through the prism of Prospero's control. Shakespeare further relies upon the use of binaries to reflect the widespread proliferation of corruption within society, using diverse characters to develop his moral judgement. Finally, Shakespeare invites the audience into an exploration of the power and corruption of language, providing a metatheatrical dimension to his sophisticated and nuanced approach to the intertwined themes. Through these three tools, Shakespeare constitutes a text rife in its interrogation of power and corruption from which the audience can draw timeless moral lessons.[21]

18. This essay also uses a variety of literary, dramatic, and grammatical techniques to analyse the text. Although no one technique is inherently better than any other, a wide variety is always advantageous!

19. We're not simply saying 'Prospero controls Ariel' – we're clarifying that Prospero's control is evident in his *words* and use of language, before taking this back to the overall thesis again before the conclusion.

20. You don't have to cover every single idea again in your conclusion, but this can be a good way of ensuring all the threads of your essay tie together neatly.

21. Finally, we conclude with a point about the text as a whole, and how Shakespeare has constructed meaning.

Essay Four

QUESTION: 'The best plays mirror our human flaws and societal problems.'
To what extent is this statement accurately reflected in *The Tempest*?

ESSAY	COMMENTS
INTRODUCTION The most enduring and valuable texts of our society possess the potential to criticise and reflect its changing audiences issues and moral dilemmas. William Shakespeare's romance *The Tempest* is clearly one such text; its ability to hold a mirror to society appealing to audiences throughout time.[1] The dramatist insightfully[2] constructs an exploration of the universal human desire to accumulate power, presenting a timeless critique of those who fall prey to their flawed ambitions. The text also appealed specifically to its contextual audience through its reflection of the power politics and ambition which plagued Jacobean era politics. But it is perhaps[3] the text's ability to lend itself to contemporary readings of the play, such as a postcolonial interpretation, which prove its enduring ability to mirror our human flaws and societal problems. Ultimately, *The Tempest's* integrity resides in its ability to reflect audiences' concerns throughout time which proves the statement integral to the text to a high extent.	1. Since this prompt is more explicitly about society and the audience, this is what our introduction focuses on to! It's a good idea to have introductions that are flexible enough to address characters, themes, audiences, or a mix of all of these depending on what the essay question dictates. 2. Though they should be used in moderation (as it's not your job to praise the author!), adverbs like this help to further your commentary about textual integrity and the importance of Shakespeare as a purposeful composer. 3. As aforementioned, the use of low modal language can help you synthesise different ideas that might otherwise be contradictory.

PARAGRAPH 1

Humans have continuously grappled with the tension between resisting the natural human urge to pursue ambition and falling prey to the natural desire to accumulate power, a struggle which Shakespeare effectively mirrors in *The Tempest*. The setting[4] of the play – a deserted island in the middle of the ocean – constitutes an open space available for the characters' conquering, as is clear through Prospero's, Stephano's, and even Gonzalo's, staking of claim to the island without thoughts of the consequences. Prospero's flawed control of the island is clear through his domination of its two inhabitants,[5] Ariel and Caliban, with Prospero's manipulation of Ariel through the invocation of his history particularly poignant: "It was mine art, / When I arrived and heard thee, that made gape / That pine, and let thee out." The possessive language in this invocation[6] indebts Ariel to Prospero, mirroring the potential for humans to fall prey to their ambitious desires, and in doing so, manipulate others along the way. But Prospero is not the only character[7] who reflects the struggle between the desire for power and the making of moral choices. Stephano, the drunken butler, upon being convinced by Caliban decides to kill Prospero in order to take control of the island, commanding Caliban, "O brave monster! Leads the way." Stephano's failure to suppress ambition is later condemned by Shakespeare through his plot's laughable failure, with Prospero dryly asking the drunken and foiled Stephano, "You'd be king o'the isle, sirrah?"

4. The vast majority of essays will jump straight into analysing characters and quotes, so occasionally stepping back to examine structural devices such as the setting can help make your analysis stand out from the crowd!

5. Now we've transitioned to talking about character relationships, and the dynamic between Prospero and Ariel/ Caliban.

6. If you need to include a slightly longer quote (e.g. multiple lines of verse), you can end the sentence there and pick up the analysis in the next sentence by commenting on what kind of language this is, and then explaining its significance.

7. Again, don't neglect the other characters! It's okay if you spend the most time on Prospero (as he is certainly an intriguing protagonist!) but you shouldn't focus on him *exclusively,* as there are really important things to be said for each of the other main characters too. You can even use less central characters (like Stephano here) as supplementary evidence to bolster your discussion.

But it is perhaps Gonzalo's musing about how he would rule the island which most alarmingly mirrors[8] this human flaw and societal problem, since he is characterised by Shakespeare as the good character, with Prospero describing him as a "noble Neapolitan." His monologue, which harkens back to Montaigne's essay, *Of Cannibals*,[9] outlines how Gonzalo would rule, 'Had I plantation of this isle.' His declaration that, "'I'th'commonwealth I would by contraries / Execute all things," reflects[10] that even morally sound characters can fall prey to the natural human desire to pursue power, thus mirroring a universal human concern and securing the text's status as one of the canon's most insightful plays.

PARAGRAPH 2
Shakespeare's amplification of power politics is not just a universal concern, but would have appealed particularly to his contextual Jacobean audience,[11] given its mirroring of key societal problems of the time. The playwright's exploration of the consequences and immorality of usurpation reflected contextual concerns about the monarchy and succession of power, thus consolidating the play's value. While monarchies are no longer as powerful in our modern context,[12] *The Tempest's* contextual audience would have recognised Antonio's, Sebastian's. and Alonso's disturbance of the natural order through their usurpation of Prospero as a deeply flawed act, which is later confirmed in Ariel's harpy speech in which he declares: "you are three men of sin." This monosyllabic condemnation bluntly reflects the importance of usurpation as a Jacobean societal issue and is furthered by the impacts that guilt has on the courtiers.[13]

8. This subtle reincorporation of a key word from the prompt reminds the assessor that we are maintaining our focus on the topic.
9. If you are analysing any allusions or intertextuality, just ensure you keep things brief, as you need to spend as much time as possible talking about your set text, not the superfluous background information.
10. Verbs like this help us instantly explain the importance and effect of quotes.
11. For any prompt that calls upon you to talk about the audience, you can acknowledge the potential differences between modern audiences and the audience of Shakespeare's time.
12. These points help contribute to our understanding of the text's universality.
13. This is an insightful point about the flaws of particular characters in the play.

In *The Tempest,* guilt manifests as a degradation of sanity, something which Gonzalo highlights in his reflection on the three usurpers: "All three of them are desperate. Their great guilt, / Like poison given tow ork a great time after, / Now 'gins to bit the spirits." This reflection is amplified by Alonso's devastation by the harpy monologue, in which he is forced to confront his sins. His guilt has affected him so deeply he admits he wants to commit suicide in order to join his son,[14] who he believes dead, delivering the devastating rhyming couplet, "I'll seek him deeper than e'er plummet sounded, / And with him there lie mudded." The sense of finality bestowed in these lines by the rhyme reinforces the moral problem of usurpation,[15] a key societal problem in The Tempest's context. Thus, Shakespeare's[16] nuanced exploration of power politics and its effects mirrors Jacobean flaws and concerns, consolidating the play's value in its own time, therefore reflecting the statement to a high extent.

PARAGRAPH 3
But it is ultimately a text's ability to transcend its contextual audience and mirror human flaws and societal problems important to new audiences which proves its brilliance, something proven by a postcolonial reading of *The Tempest.* In our contemporary world,[17] the colonisation efforts conducted in Shakespeare's time are often viewed as a moral flaw and key societal problem of the time, with many postcolonial scholars rereading texts, such as *The Tempest,* to draw out criticisms and reflections of colonial relations. This lens is highly applicable to *The Tempest,* revealing the problematic dynamic between Prospero and Caliban, thus mirroring key flaws and problems important to a modern audience.

14. You don't have to explain the summative details of the plot, but you *do* have to explain things like the characters' intentions and motivations, as these are matters of interpretation, and require justification!
15. This is a great analysis of how language creates this meaning.
16. As always, try to end your paragraph with a phrase like 'Thus, Shakespeare...' as this forces you to 'zoom out.'
17. Here, we have a further investigation of the differences between how the Jacobean audience and modern-day audiences may view *The Tempest* differently.

This mirror is constructed through the contrast between Caliban's reflection on when Prospero first came to the island: "Thou strok'st me, and made much of me; wouldst give me / Water with berries in't and teach me how / To name the bigger light... And then I loved thee," and Prospero's current treatment of Caliban, often referring to him as his "slave." Furthermore, through a postcolonial reading,[18] the problematic philosophical justification of colonisation – the civilising mission[19] – is revealed. While it is now considered a flaw, at the time it was a valid explanation of colonisation, as clear in Prospero's efforts to "teach" Caliban his Western ways and abandoning him when he is unable to reject his intrinsic "savagery." This mirroring of a key societal problem[20] is particularly apparent in Prospero's acknowledgement in the final act of Caliban as his responsibility: "this thing of darkness I acknowledge mine." Through a postcolonial reading, this admission reflects Prospero's belief he has failed to "civilise" Caliban, as clear through his usurpation attempt, and must acknowledge responsibility. This reflection of human flaws and societal problems relevant and important to a modern audience highlights the text's enduring relevance and confirms the high importance of the statement to *The Tempest*.

18. When you invoke things like a postcolonial lens, try to develop it over the course of multiple sentences and examples. Rather than being a 'buzzword' you include once and then move on from, this kind of interpretation requires a bit of work to justify, but the marker is sure to reward you if you put in the effort!
19. You'll also likely find it easier to talk about postcolonial readings when you use related terminology like this.
20. Again, we are consistently using this language straight from the essay question as a testament to how directly we are engaging with the prompt.

CONCLUSION

The best plays possess an innate ability to hold up a mirror to humanity's failings and societal problems in order to provide a comprehensive critique and didactic experience,[21] something crucial to *The Tempest's* enduring value. Ultimately, the play's reflection of the universal struggle to resist the human ambition, its exploration of power politics which resonate with its contextual audience, and its ability to be reinterpreted through the postcolonial lens and reveal key societal problems important to a modern audience proves the statement reflected accurately in *The Tempest* to a high extent.

21. Remarks like this are invaluable in establishing your thesis. It's sometimes tempting to rush through your conclusion (especially in exam conditions where there are time constraints), but try to pace yourself so that you can end on a high note!